SAY yes TO LIFE

SAY yes TO LIFE

A Book of Thoughts for Better Living

SIDNEY GREENBERG

Introduction by Andrew M. Greeley

Crown Publishers, Inc.   New York

Published by Crown Publishers, Inc., One Park Avenue, New York, New York
10016 and simultaneously in Canada by General Publishing Company Limited

Manufactured in the United States of America

Greenberg. Sidney. 1917–
    Say yes to life.

    1. Conduct of life—Addresses. essays. lectures.
2. Sermons. American—Jewish authors. 3. Sermons.
Jewish—United States. I. Title.
BJ1581.2.G69 1982   296.7′4   82-5133
ISBN 0-517-54653-1   AACR2

Design by Joanna Nelson

10 9 8 7 6 5 4 3 2 1

First Edition

To
Hilda
who has helped me
SAY YES TO LIFE
for forty years

Introduction

I have often thought that the Code of Canon Law, the Talmud, or some important document ought to establish three writing requirements for anyone seeking certification as a religious leader. These are that the person would have written:

1. sixteen sonnets
2. one novel
3. a weekly newspaper column on religious matters for an entire year

It would not be necessary that any of these efforts be published. Just by doing the writing, however, the candidate for the ministry would have learned:

1. to think in pictures rather than in propositions
2. to tell stirring stories rather than less-inspired nonfiction
3. to reduce a good idea to seven hundred nice concrete words

I suspect that Rabbi Greenberg may be pretty good at sonnet singing and tale spinning, but I especially want to pay this collection of his columns from the *Philadelphia Inquirer* what may be the ultimate compliment from one clergy person to another: I hope no one in any of the congregations to which I speak will ever read this book, for I intend to steal liberally from it in my own preaching. Higher praise than this there cannot be.

Most of us in the ministry don't realize who our real competitors are: Tom Brokaw, Jane Pauley, Mike Royko, Mike Wallace, Irma Bombeck, Art Buchwald, Ann Landers, Russell Baker. Since we have, on Saturday or Sunday, a more or less captive audience, we feel we can do just as we wish—wander a bit, blow a little hard, try to sound like scholars and theologians, and try to impress the vast number of Ph.D.s who we fancy crowd our churches every week. And, mostly, we get away with it. Our people may nod, but they come back because they want religion, even if they have to put up with our tiresome sermons to get it. If people don't like a columnist they don't read him, and after a time, and one way or another, they let the editor know it. It's a lot harder to do that to your rabbi or your priest.

The clerical columnist is less protected, competing as he does in the marketplace of communicators. He has just seven hundred words to make his points each week. He must be utterly professional about gaining attention in the first paragraph, in sustaining attention in subsequent paragraphs, and then in driving home his point—sometimes with the delicacy of a spring breeze, sometimes with the force of a hammerblow—in the final sentences.

If you think it's easy, you might wish to try it some time.

Rabbi Greenberg has tried it, and obviously with enormous success. I am sure he would tell you it's not all that easy, and as one who plays the same game to some extent, I would back him up. The Rabbi is, in fact, very good at the game, very good indeed. I suspect that he takes a bit of heat from other clergymen for the attention his column gets and perhaps for the fact that he tries so heroically to reduce a heritage to seven hundred words.

Perhaps the Rabbi wouldn't say it, but I'll say it for him: Any heritage that cannot be reduced to seven hundred concrete words on a Sunday morning in the *Inquirer* is not a heritage I'd want to be part of. And any religious teacher who cannot accomplish this when called upon to do so needs a lot of professional updating.

What I especially like about Rabbi Greenberg's columns is that they are thoroughly Jewish. You'd never for a moment think they were written by a priest or by a Methodist minister. Some religious columns try to offer thought compounded out of all the heritages and succeed only in writing out of none. In a misguided quest for comprehensiveness, they offer us only the blandest teaching. They try to speak to everyone and speak, in fact, to no one.

Precisely because he is so fully and so richly Jewish, Rabbi Greenberg can speak meaningfully to the rest of us who are in different strains of what I believe to be the same great heritage.

Keep it up, Rabbi Greenberg. Say yes not only to life but to continuing to offer us, through your columns, this good and useful way of exploring and understanding it.

ANDREW M. GREELEY
Feast of St. Andrew
1981

A Word to the Reader

Any author who is familiar with Koheleth's weary complaint that "of the making of books there is no end" (Ecclesiastes 12:12) instinctively feels impelled to justify himself against the charge of the biblical cynic. Why indeed another book?

Koheleth's own actions provide the answer. His unhappiness over the multiplicity of books did not prevent him from adding one of his own. And it is fortunate for posterity that he was not inhibited. The Bible would be a poorer collection if he had taken seriously his own protestations. One need not necessarily possess his literary gifts to follow his example. If only those birds sang who have the most beautiful voices, the forest would be almost silent.

In truth, this book did not start out as a book at all. Its brief essays were originally written for the readers of the *Philadelphia Inquirer,* and their intended audience was not without significant influence on their tone and character. Let me explain.

By a happy coincidence, this volume appears as I am marking the completion of four decades of rabbinic service. During these forty years I have served only one congregation, Temple Sinai in Dresher, Pennsylvania, and I have been the only rabbi the congregation has had in its history. This relationship is unique if not unprecedented.

One of the chief functions of the contemporary pulpit rabbi is to interpret the insights of a rich and ancient tradition and to make them relevant to the concerns, the dilemmas, and the lives of his congregants. The rabbi's chief vehicle of communication is the spoken sermon delivered on sabbaths, festivals, and holy days. Given the time and place in which these messages are delivered and the composition of the congregation to which they are addressed, it is understandable that the sermon themes, illustrations, and exhortations will have a distinctive Jewish flavor.

When I was invited to write a column for the newspaper I realized that the mixed backgrounds of my readers required that my messages take on a more universal character even while they conveyed what I regard to be essentially Jewish perspectives and values. That these columns won wide and friendly acceptance by people of all faiths—and some of no established faith—has been a source of immense gratification. The reader response has more than amply rewarded me for the effort that went into the columns. That response has also provided the encouragement to bring the columns together between the covers of this book. For that encouragement I am deeply grateful.

My genuine gratitude goes also to Nat Wartels, the chairman of Crown Publishers, who brought out my first volume, *A Treasury of Comfort,* some twenty-eight years ago and now—some twenty volumes having intervened—he again expresses his faith in my work. His confidence is a treasured gift.

Naomi Kleinberg, a member of the editorial staff of Crown Publishers, has worked with me in the preparation of this volume and has cheerfully put at my disposal the full range of her many literary talents. The book is a better one for her attention and I am richer for her friendship.

Lee Kovacs, my secretary, has been unrelenting in "nudging" me to publish the columns in book form. Ultimately I found it easier to make the effort than to put up with her prodding. I thank her for her persistence and also, not so incidentally, for deciphering my hieroglyphic script and translating it into the typed word.

Together with Lee, two friends, Betty Shusterman and Gert Silnutzer, faithful members of our office staff, were always ready to read and react to the first draft of every column. Their opinions were genuinely valuable because they had the courage to be honest. They, too, have earned my warm gratitude.

In a special way I am also indebted to my good friends of Temple Sinai. In a very real sense these essays are as much their property as mine. Their needs have served as my motivations. Their predicaments have been my texts. From the crucible of their experiences I have distilled most of my themes. Above all, their unfailing support over the years has enabled me to devote a portion of my energies to writing for the larger audiences to which this book and those that preceded it have been addressed.

My wife, to whom I have dedicated this book, has been a very vital part of my ministry. Her service to the congregation has been more noteworthy than my own because her immense contributions were made voluntarily. Her sensitivity to human need, her compassion for the friendless, the lonely, the bereaved, have done much to convert a large congregation into an intimate family. I can only wonder whether her acts of kindness have not done more than my words to help so many "say yes to life."

I release this book with the fervent prayer that "words that come from the heart may enter the heart." May the reader find in its pages some added encouragement to "say yes to life." If it accomplishes that purpose, it will provide more than adequate recompense for the labor of love out of which it was born.

SIDNEY GREENBERG
Dresher, Pennsylvania
1981

To Live All the Days of Our Lives

Some years ago a religious sect adopted as its motto these words: "Millions now living will never die," whereupon one observer remarked, "Yes, but the tragedy is that millions now living are already dead but do not know it."

The rabbinic teachers may have been pointing in the same direction in their comment on the biblical narrative that tells of the death of the two sons of Aaron, Nadav and Avihu. The sages said that the young men had suffered a peculiar kind of death: "Their souls were consumed; their bodies remained intact."

Had the sages filled out the coroner's report, it might have read: "Biologically sound, spiritually dead." The ancient rabbis confirmed here a moral verdict that they rendered more explicitly in another passage: "The wicked even in life are considered dead."

Much is being written these days on the question of when true biological death sets in. When the heart stops beating? When the brain stops functioning? But what is the status of the human being when the soul shrivels and the spirit withers?

At a time when there is growing popular interest in a belief in life after death and a widely publicized book is entitled *Life After Life,* should we not each give more attention to the question "How about life during life?" Are we truly and fully alive, not only biologically, but spiritually as well?

Sinclair Lewis was a professed atheist. Once he engaged in a public debate in Kansas City on whether or not God exists. He finished his presentation with the dramatic challenge: "If there is a God, let him strike me dead now." He waited a few moments, nothing happened, and he marched triumphantly off the platform.

The following morning the *Kansas City Times* printed an editorial response to Lewis. Of course, it said, God did strike Lewis dead even though he did not seem to be aware of it. His spiritual demise was reflected in his despair about the value of life, in his cynical contempt for people, in his sneering egotism, and in his

1

waning literary powers. It was another case of a human being who was biologically sound, spiritually dead.

A colleague once blessed his young grandson in these words: "My child, may you live all the days of your life." To live all the days of our lives is to live fully, with our whole being, with heart and mind and spirit. It means cultivating all our God-given resources for inner growth. It means being alive to the beauty of the world and to the wonder and the miracle of being part of it. It means becoming ever more sensitive to the abiding joys of sharing, the extravagant rewards of loving, the bountiful harvests of believing.

It means, in the words of the Hebrew prophet, "to act justly, to love mercy, and to walk humbly with your God" (Micah 6:8).

Making the Most of Our Best

A few months after Walter Davis, thirty-three, divorced his wife, Barbara, he enlisted the aid of a computer dating service in his search for a new mate. He filled out a lengthy questionnaire in which he provided a great deal of information about himself and about the qualities he sought in a wife.

The computer ran through thirty thousand prospects and then came up with four names. The first name on the list was that of Barbara, his former wife! She had filed a similar form with the same mate-selecting computer.

This is a story worth pondering. For one thing, it might give pause to some people headed for the overcrowded divorce courts. Before they dissolve a marriage, dismantle a home, and disrupt a family, they could profitably ask themselves whether with more patience, effort, and greater determination they could not make a go of their marriage.

Perhaps Walter's experience can slow them down long enough for them to ask whether what they need is to change their mates or to change themselves. Do they require a change of circumstance or a change of attitude? Is the answer in the computer or within themselves?

These questions are not confined to people who find themselves in a shaky marriage. They touch all of us at the point in our lives at which we are tempted to believe that we really could be happy if our circumstances were other than what they are. "Ah, if I lived in another place, in another time; if only I were attractive or rich; if only I had different parents or different genes; if only things were different."

Becky Sharp in Thackeray's *Vanity Fair* excused her loose morals by saying, "I think I could be a good woman if I had 5,000 pounds a year." Becky was kidding herself, and so are we when we blame our circumstances and shirk our responsibility to make maximum use of the opportunities at hand. Those who find fulfillment in life are those who change what should and can be changed, accept what cannot be changed, and go on from there.

This, I believe, is the meaning of that spectacular encounter Moses experienced at the burning bush. There he was in a bleak, desolate wilderness when he heard the divine command: "Remove your shoes from your feet, for the place on which you stand is holy ground." Holy ground! Here, in this barren, dreary spot? Yes, Moses. Here in this miserable place you can find a mission that will give meaning and purpose to your life.

Elizabeth Barrett Browning had that biblical episode in mind when she wrote:

> *Earth's crammed with heaven*
> *And every common bush afire with God;*
> *But only he who sees, takes off his shoes,*
> *The rest sit round it and pluck blackberries.*

When we learn to look upon the humble ground on which we stand as holy ground, we have acquired the greatest encouragement we need to fertilize it and make it productive. We discover the poetry that is ambushed in the prosaic, the glory that is embedded in the commonplace, the opportunity that is hidden in the thicket of thorn bushes. If we wait until circumstances are precisely right for us to achieve and accomplish something, then nothing ever will be achieved or accomplished. Neither we nor circumstances are ever precisely right. Each of us has heartaches and pains, limitations and handicaps. Each of us has burdens to carry and obstacles to overcome. And as Emerson reminded us, there is a crack in everything that God has made.

Moses himself was a stammerer and a stutterer, a refugee from justice, a member of an enslaved people. Circumstances were scarcely ideal for the assignment he was given. But a grateful humanity holds him in warm remembrance because he did the very best he could, and in the least likely of places he discovered holy ground.

Nor was Moses the only person to achieve mightily despite forbidding circumstances. Lord Byron had a clubfoot; Robert Louis Stevenson had tuberculosis; Charles Darwin was an invalid;

Thomas Edison and Ludwig van Beethoven were deaf; George Washington Carver was a black slave; Abraham Lincoln was born in a log cabin to parents who could neither read nor write; and Helen Keller could neither see nor hear.

The verdict of history is clear. Among the humble and great alike, those who achieve success do so not because fate and circumstance are especially kind to them. Often the reverse is true. They succeed because they do not whine over their fate but take whatever has been given to them and go on to make the most of their best.

It Is Human Nature to Change Human Actions

The holiest time on the Jewish calendar is the ten-day period that begins with Rosh Hashanah, the Jewish New Year, and ends with Yom Kippur, the Day of Atonement. These ten days are days of introspection, a time for looking inward, a time to examine our achievements and our failures, our goals and our guilts, our successes and our sins. To what end this annual spiritual stock taking?

We are urged to undergo moral self-examination so that we might address ourselves to our faults and our transgressions and strive to eliminate them in the year ahead.

But can we in fact overcome our faults? Are they not so deeply engraved in our nature that we are only deluding ourselves when we believe we can eradicate them? Is not the popular adage true: "You can't change human nature"?

The answer of Judaism is to reject any and every kind of fatalism that denies us the freedom to choose our way and to strike out in new directions. We are not enslaved by impersonal nature, nor are we subject to the influence of the stars or planets.

Moreover, as Abba Hillel Silver, a great twentieth-century rabbi and scholar, has written:

Man is not forever doomed to the errors and the consequences of his past conduct. He is free to repent and through repentance to nullify the evil influences of his past over him. Repentance means the opportunity of a new start, the chance to correct what man had left crooked, to fill that which is wanting in one's life.

To each of us, these holy days bring the reassuring message that we are not eternally chained by what we have been. We can throw off the tyranny of enslaving habits. Our tomorrow can be freed from the shackles of yesterday.

These days mightily affirm that we can conquer the selfishness that shrinks us, the prejudice that blinds us, the indifference that dehumanizes us, the envy that gnaws at us, the greed that impels us.

"How do we know that a man's sins have been forgiven?" asked a Hassidic rabbi. And he answered: "When he no longer commits the sin." We are free to break with what we have been, to become what in the depths of our hearts we know we can be.

And in this struggle we are not alone. God is our ally. God who gave us the power to repent helps us in this endeavor.

Our sages picture God as saying to us: "If you open the door of repentance only as wide as a needle's eye, I will open it wide enough for carriages and wagons to pass through."

You can't change human nature? Perhaps. But it is human nature to change human actions, and that is what these days are all about.

Taking a Look at Ourselves

The story is told about a gung-ho drill sergeant who always demanded the highest and the best from his soldiers. One day he stared in pained disbelief at a sloppy squad of new recruits wearing their uniforms for the first time. For a moment the sergeant was speechless with rage. Then he blurted out, "Just step out here and look at yourselves!"

The sergeant's indignation obviously interfered with the clarity of his language, but his order embodied a significant truth. There is a time when all of us should step out and look at ourselves.

The beginning of a new year is an excellent time to do just that. When the merrymaking and its aftereffects are over, we have to settle down to the sober business of living. The new year comes to us carrying a basket filled with opportunities and challenges. Above all, it urges us to step out and take a real hard look at ourselves.

One of the convicted coconspirators in the Watergate scandal made a remarkable confession: "I have lived fifty years of my life without ever really coming to grips with the very basic questions of what is and what is not important to me; what is and what is not right and wrong; what is and what is not valuable and worthwhile."

He was saying, in effect, that at the age of fifty, he had not yet taken a real hard look at himself.

In addition to the "very basic questions" he mentioned, here are some others we might each ask ourselves as we survey the years that have come and gone:

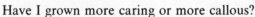

Have I grown more caring or more callous?
Have I become more forgiving or more vengeful?
Have I become more tolerant or more critical?
Have I become more generous or more self-centered?
Have I striven to become better or only better off?
Have I held on to my principles or have I abandoned them?

Have I changed for the better or for the worse?
Have I grown as a person or have I become smaller?

Lewis Mumford, the American philosopher and historian, calls us "unfinished animals." We have the capacity to work on the raw material with which we start life, and we need never stop improving it, transforming it, perfecting it.

When the time comes, each year, to launch ourselves into another new year, we might be lavishly rewarded if we took a real hard look at ourselves. It could help to make us happier with what we see, eventually, when the new year's grown old and come to an end.

Check Your Chains

Passover, the Jewish festival of freedom, brings a message of hope to people everywhere who still live under dictators, despots, and totalitarian monarchs. To those of us who are uniquely privileged to live in a democracy, Passover brings a challenge.

Can we in our own lives experience an exodus from the bondage in which so many tyrants hold us? Is it not true that we who lived in a land of freedom are still subject to enslavement by inner despots—just like the pharaohs of old—who hold us in chains?

Some time ago, a punk-rock performer was in jail awaiting trial on charges of stabbing his girl friend to death. Then he was released on bail. To celebrate his regained freedom, he went to a party where he wanted a real high, so he doped himself with heroin. Apparently he took an overdose, and the next day they were unable to arouse him. He was dead. Question: When he was released from jail and remained enslaved to heroin, was he really free?

On the day after the first snow of one winter season, a manufacturer of tire chains ran an ad in the newspapers that urged, "Check Your Chains!" Passover also urges us to check our chains, the chains that keep us in bondage and prevent us from exercising our human freedom.

Some of us are chained by blind prejudice that keeps us from seeing people as they really are.

Some of us are enslaved by tyrannical habits that we have pampered into power and now rule over us with an iron fist.

Some of us are kept in bondage by ignorance and superstition that stunt the mind and suffocate the spirit.

Some of us are fettered by fears and anxieties that disturb our days and haunt our nights.

Some of us are imprisoned by greed and mean ambition, by status seeking and phony values.

Some of us are enlisted in forced labor to the slave master called "success" that makes exorbitant demands and gives paltry rewards.

10

Some of us are shackled by jealousy that sours us, hatred that poisons us, and self-doubt that disables us.

We have a distressing sense of self-recognition in the words of James Oppenheim, the American poet and novelist:

> *They set the slave free, striking off his chains,*
> *Then he was as much of a slave as ever.*
> *He was still chained to servility,*
> *He was still manacled to indolence and sloth,*
> *He was still bound by fear and superstition,*
> *By ignorance, suspicion and savagery.*
> *His slavery was not in the chains,*
> *But in himself.*

What are we doing to dethrone the inner pharaohs who hold us in bondage?

Mark Twain told the exasperating but encouraging story of a man who spent long, hard years in prison only to walk out one fine morning when he discovered that the doors had never been locked!

We who spend years imprisoned by the chains we ourselves have forged can, if we try, open the doors and walk out into the sunshine of freedom to which Passover summons us.

Who Is a Hero?

While the festival of Passover is a distinctly Jewish holiday, the biblical narrative out of which it emerged contains a truth that can enrich people of all faiths and of none. After enduring the visitation on his people of ten brutal plagues, Pharaoh is at last going to release the Israelite slaves from Egyptian bondage. But, as we read the story carefully, we realize that their chains have not disappeared—now Pharaoh wears them!

It is the pharaoh who is enslaved—by his hunger for power and his greed for possessions. He cannot break his habit of manipulating people as though they were so many bricks. Again and again, as each plague is visited upon his hapless people, he agrees to let the slaves go, so that the plague may be lifted. But no sooner is the plague removed than he suffers a relapse. His heart grows hard again, to use the biblical phrase. And even after the last bloody plague persuades him to release the slaves, he soon reverts to his old ways and pursues the Israelites to his watery grave. The chains of the Israelites were ultimately broken, but the pharaoh never freed himself.

The American poet Edwin Markham may have been thinking of Pharaoh when he wrote the quatrain he calls "Even Scales":

> *The robber is robbed by his riches,*
> *The tyrant is dragged by his chain;*
> *The schemer is snared by his cunning;*
> *The slayer lies dead by the slain.*

Alphonse de Lamartine, the nineteenth-century French poet and politician, spoke directly to our theme when he declared: "Man never fastened one end of a chain around the neck of his brother, that God did not fasten the other end around the neck of the oppressors."

Most of us in this land of freedom are neither oppressors nor oppressed in the political sense. Nevertheless, too many of us are slaves. And the most distressing part of our enslavement is that

12

the chains we wear we have forged for ourselves, as the pharaoh forged his own.

Some of us are the slaves of destructive habits and crippling fears. Some are imprisoned by unworthy ambitions and shabby pursuits. Some are held captive by the relentless drive for power or wealth. Others are chained by suspicions, superstitions, prejudices. We permit a host of inner tyrants to keep us in bondage.

As we read once again the ancient biblical drama of liberation, we are powerfully reminded that God wants each of us to be free. He summons us to be masters—not of others, but of ourselves.

"Who is a hero?" the Jewish sages asked. Their answer: "He who masters himself."

Everybody's Doing It

In Eugene Ionesco's play *Rhinoceros,* a human being actually turns into a rhinoceros. Indeed, before the play is over, all but one of the characters have undergone the same transformation.

The key sentence in the play is spoken by the heroine, who witnessed a man turned into an animal. "Just before he became a beast," she reports, "his last human words were 'We must move with the times.'"

The playwright has sounded a warning our generation needs very much to hear. One of the most serious threats to our humanity stems from our misguided desire to "move with the times," to be what everybody else is, to do what everyone else is doing.

To permit what everybody else is doing to determine what we should be doing may find us doing what nobody should be doing. That is a sure way to become one of the herd, to surrender our human uniqueness, and to risk becoming a rhinoceros.

The Bible raises the same warning flag where it tells us: "You shall not follow a multitude to do evil" (Exodus 23:2).

No matter how many people steal, stealing remains wrong. No matter how many people are corrupt, corruption remains wrong. No matter how many people betray public trust, that action remains wrong. The fact that any misdeed becomes popular does not make it permissible. The problem of evil is not solved by multiplication.

Moving with the times does not mean surrendering timeless truths or abandoning the accumulated decencies of the centuries.

Moreover, whenever any unworthy action is justified on the ground that "everybody's doing it," we ought to pause and reflect that, as a matter of fact, not everybody's doing it.

There are a host of people day in and day out living by the enduring values, abiding by the time-honored traditions, measuring up to the cherished standards of truth and goodness and integrity. They are the solid little pegs that keep this world of ours together. And they are more numerous than the newspaper head-

14

lines would lead us to believe. Crime gets all the attention, goodness goes unreported.

There is nothing sensational about honesty or loyalty or fidelity because, if the truth be told, they are really what most people believe in and practice.

The old adage counsels us: "When in Rome do as the Romans do." The Bible would add—provided that what the Romans are doing ought to be done. Otherwise, "You shall not follow a multitude to do evil."

On Blaming Circumstances

A history-making lawsuit involved a twenty-four-year-old man from Boulder, Colorado, who sued his parents to the tune of $350,000. He accused them of "psychological malparenting" which means, translated into simpler language, messing up his life.

He was saying in effect that all that has gone wrong in his life, his failure to make a go of things, is not his fault. He had no part in his failure. He was the innocent, passive victim of the mistakes of others.

There is a widespread tendency today to evade responsibility for our actions. We are pictured as the victims of genes, reflexes, complexes, passions, glands. We are seen as mere puppets being manipulated by massive forces that buffet us about and which you and I are impotent to control.

This whole philosophy of evasion was neatly summed up in a cartoon in which a little boy complains to his father: "Mother is always blaming me for everything that I do."

There is, therefore, a sobering and much-needed corrective sounded in the oft-quoted biblical verse: "Behold, I set before you this day a blessing and a curse" (Deuteronomy 11:26).

A set of alternatives is placed before us, and we are urged to choose the blessing and reject the curse. We are free moral agents able to distinguish good from evil, and capable of choosing good over evil.

This is not to deny the vital influence of our biological inheritance, our childhood experiences, our environmental conditioning. Those things are real and powerful, but the human will is even more powerful.

For we are not only shaped by our environment; we shape it.

Our friend in Colorado did not succeed in his lawsuit against his parents. But his bigger failure, it seems to me, was blaming *them* for his failure instead of taking responsibility for his own life and trying to make the most of it.

Failure can be helpful if we learn from it the things that don't work. But failure leaves us none the wiser if we look for scape-goats.

And no person succeeds in any enterprise until he takes respon-sibility for his choices, until he knows with unwavering certainty that he has choices, and that upon the outcome of those choices his entire destiny will depend.

"People," wrote George Bernard Shaw, "are always blaming their circumstances for what they are. I can't believe in circum-stances. The people who get on in this world are the people who get up and look for the circumstances they want, and if they can't find them, make them."

On Running Away from Ourselves

There is a running boom in this country, not only on the tracks and city streets but also in the bookstores.

One book on running has enjoyed a long run on the national best-seller list. At least thirty other books on running have been published. Running enthusiasts even contend that running can provide a spiritual "high."

After a 26-mile, 385-yard marathon in New York's Central Park, a newspaper ran an enthusiastic lead editorial entitled "Inside, Every One of Us Is a Distance Runner."

That title sent my thoughts running on a somewhat different track. It reminded me that running is an ancient enterprise, as old as the human race (no pun intended). I am thinking not of the kind of running that makes us more fit to face life but of the kind of running that is an effort to evade life, to escape from its burdens, to get away from it all.

The most celebrated runner in the Bible is Jonah, the central character in the tale of Jonah and the whale, which I consider a whale of a tale, to be taken seriously but not literally.

God sent Jonah to preach a message of repentance to the inhabitants of Nineveh, the capital of Israel's bitter foe, Syria. Jonah doesn't like the idea at all. Why should he care about these Gentiles, and Gentile enemies yet! So what does Jonah do? "And Jonah arose to run to Tarshish away from God" (Jonah 1:3).

Jonah begins the longest race of all, running away from God. Instead of setting out for Nineveh, he takes a slow boat to Tarshish. This kind of marathon did not begin with Jonah and did not end with him. Inside, every one of us is . . . a little like Jonah. We each have our own Ninevehs from which we want to run.

We want to run from unpleasant duties, from nagging responsibilities, from life's complexities and confusions. We want to run from harsh realities, from our fears and anxieties, from an accusing conscience. We want to run from the boredom and bewilderment of existence.

And there are many ships we board as we head for our own

little Tarshish. Some get turned on and some get turned off. Some drop out and some cop out. Some develop asthma and some get headaches. Some get lost in petty pleasures and some in the pursuit of fun.

But if there is one lesson that Jonah teaches us, it is that there is no running away; wherever we go we take ourselves along. God finds Jonah even in the belly of the whale. The only way to "get away" from ourselves is to effect a change within ourselves. What we need is not a change of scene but a change of soul.

It is only when Jonah finally goes to Nineveh, when he accepts and discharges his responsibility, when he stands up to life, that he saves both Nineveh and himself. He has stopped running.

In our own time, Dag Hammarskjöld, the great secretary general of the United Nations, once put the truth simply: "Life demands from you only the strength you possess. Only one feat is possible—not to have run away."

Humbled by the Stars

Earliest Jewish history is dominated by the towering figure of Moses.

It was he who kindled in the heavy hearts of a downtrodden slave people the yearning to be free. It was he who led them triumphantly out of Egypt. It was he who served as God's agent for the revelation at Sinai. It was he who led his people for forty years through the fierce and forbidding desert.

Moses possessed many noteworthy qualities, and the Bible could have singled out any number of them for praise, and yet there is only one direct compliment that Scripture pays Moses: "The man Moses was very humble, above all the men who were on the face of the earth" (Numbers 12:3). Humility is the quality, above all others, to which the Torah called direct attention.

But ours is a society singularly uncongenial to the flowering of humility. This is the age that has created the high-pressure publicity agent and promoted advertising into one of America's major industries.

Neither of these developments was triggered by an excess of modesty. Indeed, if a sense of humility ever descended on Madison Avenue, many a publicity agent would be stricken with total disability and we would probably never know again the touching musical tributes to soapsuds or the heartwarming poems in praise of dog food.

In recommending a man for a job or an applicant for admission to a school, we are likely to call attention to his reliability, industry, integrity, intelligence. Rarely, if ever, would we think of including humility among his attractive qualities, for humility in our time is almost a lost virtue.

Yet humility is one of the dominant features of the spiritual profile drawn by religion. Humility is the climax of the prophet Micah's eloquent summation of man's highest duties: "What does the Lord require of you? Only to do justice, to love mercy, and to walk humbly with your God" (Micah 6:8).

Perhaps here is the secret to the rediscovery of humility—to

20

walk humbly with God. Before God, how small we all are! When we walk with God it must be humbly.

For what, after all, is the music of a Heifetz before Him who taught the brooks to murmur, the leaves to whisper, the wind to howl, birds to sing, and babies to cry? How impressive is a Shakespeare compared to the Divine Playwright whose dramas touch everything and whose cast of characters includes every human being? How significant is the brush of a Picasso alongside the One who paints sunsets daily and touches the leaves of autumn with intoxicating colors? How large is our knowledge compared with the Infinite Wisdom? How big is our goodness alongside the unspeakable mercy of God?

A mountain shames a molehill until they are both humbled by the stars. Phillips Brooks, the nineteenth-century clergyman, was dispensing quite sound spiritual advice when he said, "The true way to be humble is not to stoop until you are smaller than yourself but to stand at your real height against some higher nature that will show you what the real smallness of your greatness is."

Converting an Inferno into a
Place of Beauty

One of the highlights of Israel's thirtieth anniversary celebration was a mammoth Independence Day concert. It featured Zubin Mehta conducting the Israel Philharmonic Orchestra, Isaac Stern, Daniel Barenboim, Jean-Pierre Rampal, Leontyne Price, Itzhak Perlman—one of the greatest assemblages of musicians ever to gather on one platform.

Impressive as the concert itself was the place where it was held: the Hinnom Valley just outside the walls of the Old City of Jerusalem. The valley is a small ravine where, the Bible tells us, idolaters used to burn their children as offerings to their god Moloch. Because of this horrendous association, the Hinnom Valley, or Gehinnom in Hebrew, became in Jewish thought the hell where sinners are punished for their misdeeds while on earth.

I found the idea of staging the Independence Day concert in the Hinnom Valley enormously suggestive. To me it said that it is possible to go into hell and convert the inferno into a place of beauty and celebration.

Surely grief is a terrible inferno, and yet, despite its forbidding countenance, sorrow possesses great potential power to expand our lives, to enlarge our vision, and to deepen our understanding.

Through the portals of sorrow we can enter into the suffering of others. Our human compassion is kindled. Our sympathies are awakened. Grief can also help purge us of pettiness and selfishness. It can elicit from us powers of fortitude and patience.

The abundance of elegiac poetry and music in world culture points up another benevolent service that suffering frequently renders. Where we do not permit it to embitter us or crush us, it often arouses latent powers of creativity by which the human spirit transmutes suffering into soul, adversity into artistry, pain into poetry.

It is quite possible to emulate those of whom the psalmist wrote: "They pass through a valley of tears and convert it into a life-giving fountain" (Psalms 84:7).

In Israel there is a rare cactus plant on which there grows an exquisitely lovely flower. The flower is called "Queen of the Night" because it has the strange characteristic of blooming only in the darkest part of the night. When the blackness is deepest, the Queen of the Night comes bursting out.

We can be like that flower and, in the dark night of sorrow, shine forth robed in our full human splendor, bedecked in our God-given glory.

In the valley of Hinnom we can play the most beautiful music.

Many Are Strong in the Broken Places

When Glenn Cunningham was a boy of eight, he and his brother attempted to start the fire to heat their school building. A violent kerosene explosion ensued and Glenn's legs were so badly burned that the doctors proposed amputation. His mother would not hear of it.

After six long months in the hospital, a series of extensive skin grafts, and endless hours of massaging by his mother's loving hands, Glenn began to walk and then to run to strengthen his crippled legs. He ran and he ran and he ran, until at age twenty-five he ran straight into a world record for the fastest mile—a record he was to hold for years.

The world applauded Cunningham's courage no less than his skill, for he had provided a thrilling illustration of the truth of Ernest Hemingway's words: "The world breaks everyone, and afterward many are strong in the broken places."

Indeed, there are two truths in Hemingway's statement. The first is that sooner or later we are all broken. Defeat, disappointment, sorrow, and tragedy are the common lot of all people.

If there were an X ray capable of giving us a picture of the human spirit, we would find that we all show evidence of emotional and psychic fractures. Some of us have suffered the break caused by a deep frustration—a career we sought but did not attain, a loved one we wooed but failed to win. Some of us have scars left by a haunting sense of inadequacy; by physical and mental abuse; by blasted hopes; by unrealized dreams; by losses we cannot recapture or forget.

"Man," the Bible says, "is born to trouble as surely as the sparks fly upward" (Job 5:7). Trouble is not a gate-crasher in the arena of our lives; it has a reserved seat there. Heartache has a passkey to every home in the land.

After Helen Hayes suffered the loss of her young and gifted daughter, Mary, she wrote, "When God afflicts the celebrated of the world, it is His way of saying, 'None is privileged. In my eyes all are equal.' "

24

But Hemingway talks not only of our common vulnerability to being broken; he reminds us too that we can later become strong in the broken places. Where trouble and suffering are concerned, you and I, like young Glenn, have the power not only to confront and endure them; we can use them constructively and creatively.

I say we *can* use them, not that we necessarily *do* use them. *Many* are strong in the broken places—not *all*. Some are embittered by suffering. Some are overcome by self-pity. "Why did it happen to me?" Some are resentful.

But then there are others who understand that some of the noblest human traits flourish in the soil of suffering. Compassion and kindness, fortitude and patience, sympathy and humility—these are part of the rich harvest that can ripen from the dark seeds of pain.

Robert Browning Hamilton captured a sustaining truth when he wrote:

> *I walked a mile with Sorrow,*
> *And ne'er a word said she,*
> *But, oh, the things I learned from her*
> *When Sorrow walked with me.*

Whether or not we become strong in the broken places depends ultimately on our attitude toward trouble. If we realize that suffering is our common human lot and that it can help us to grow in spirit and in understanding, then we can indeed use it to grow strong in the broken places.

Touch Me with Noble Anger

In the late 1970s, during the days of long lines at the gas pumps, one motorist saw another get into line in front of him. Some hot words were exchanged, and the fellow who was in line first got so angry he whipped out a gun and killed the other fellow.

Some teenagers at a London birthday party were celebrating rather noisily through the night. One of the disturbed neighbors got so angry he threw a firebomb into the house. Result: nine killed and thirty injured.

A few years ago a fire killed twenty-six people at Stouffer's Inn in Harrison, New York. The fire was believed to have been started by a disgruntled employee who got angry because he'd been told that he was going to be dismissed.

We read these stories and we are quick to moralize what a terrible and destructive emotion anger is. ANGER, we are reminded, is only one letter removed from DANGER. And we can sympathize fully with the little fellow whose angry outburst brought him swift punishment. "Dear God," he was later heard praying, "please take away my temper, and while you're at it, take away my father's temper too."

Our society frowns upon any display of anger. It is considered a nasty breach of social etiquette. It is viewed as evidence of a lack of self-control. And as the expression *getting mad* indicates, to be angry is often taken as a sign of madness. The Roman poet Horace defined anger as "temporary lunacy."

Despite all this, there is in fact nothing wrong with anger. It is not "bad" or "sinful"; it is as normal and as healthy as grief, love, joy, fear, sadness. Anger is a basic part of our human equipment, found earliest in infancy, as a response, for example, to frustration or rejection.

Anger that is denied an outlet is like a festering sore which can poison the body and the mind. It is the stuff of which ulcers are made. It can cause blood pressure to rise, depression to set in.

Anger that is bottled up can lead to guilt, anxiety, dangerous driving. In its ultimate form, it turns in upon oneself and can even lead to suicide. When an angry person says, "Boy, am I burned up," he may be giving an excellent description of the ravages being wrought within him by suppressed anger.

If our prisons are full of people who expressed their anger in unacceptable ways, our psychiatric hospitals are full of people who have not been able to express their anger at all.

We have to overcome our fear of expressing the anger we feel. As the late Dr. Michael J. Halberstam counseled, we have to "let ourselves really get mad." Moreover, we should express our anger "loud and clear, at the real target, complete with shouting and table-pounding if the feeling is strong enough—but please, no pounding on people."

We can go further and observe that anger, constructively channeled, can be a mighty force for good. The wheels of progress were frequently moved by the steam of anger. Moses left the security of the pharaoh's palace and threw in his lot with his miserable brothers and sisters because he was profoundly angered by injustice and oppression. Lincoln's fierce opposition to slavery was born out of anger; when he stood one day at a slave auction and saw a screaming woman being wrenched away from her husband and child, he vowed in his indignation: "That's wrong, and if I ever get a chance to hit it, I'll hit it hard."

Long ago a Hebrew sage taught that "he who conquers his anger is more to be admired than he who conquers a city." To conquer anger does not mean to try to suppress it, to be ashamed of it, to deny its legitimacy. To conquer anger means to express it at the appropriate time, in an appropriate manner.

Aristotle anticipated modern psychology when he wrote: "Anybody can become angry—that is easy; but to be angry with the right person, and to the right degree, and at the right time and for the right purpose and in the right way—that is not within everybody's power and is not easy."

Perhaps then the prayer of the little fellow is not our prayer after all. We should not ask God to take away our temper. Instead, we should ask in Shakespeare's words: "Touch me with noble anger."

Even Envy Can Be Used

Our Bible is not always a peaceful book filled with serenity, green pastures, and brotherly love. It is a book that holds up a mirror to life, reflecting its pains, its passions, its conflicts.

One such conflict is the fierce rebellion against Moses led by Korach (Numbers 16). The details of the revolt need not concern us here, but we might do well to consider the motive behind the uprising.

The Jewish sages attributed Korach's rebellion to a consuming envy. Korach, according to rabbinic tradition, was so extravagantly endowed with worldly goods that a folk expression would describe an extremely wealthy person as being "as rich as Korach."

But for all his wealth, his attention was focused not on what he had in such ample abundance but on the one thing he lacked—the leadership of the people. It was his envy of Moses that prompted him to revolt and that, ultimately, led to his destruction.

If envy had perished with Korach, it would be of little concern to us. Unhappily, however, envy, which Shakespeare called "the green sickness," is still very much with us and within us. An eighteenth-century essayist wrote that "there is but one man who can believe himself free from envy and it is he who has never examined his own heart."

Envy, it appears, is unrelated to what a person possesses. It does not depend on his status, the size of his home, the length of his car, the thickness of his investment portfolio. The Greek philosopher Diogenes lived in a tub and it was large enough for him. His contemporary, Alexander the Great, conquered the world, and before he died at the age of thirty-three he lamented that he had no more worlds to conquer. A tub was large enough for Diogenes but the world was too small for Alexander the Great.

A good antidote to envy is to pause occasionally to ask: How happy, really, is the person who possesses the object of our envy? That person may very well be tormented by his envy of someone else.

We might also draw up a list of the countless blessings that are already ours and that we habitually overlook and take for granted—health, our loved ones, food, shelter, freedom. Let one of these be threatened and we suddenly realize how fabulously rich we truly are.

If we are to resist the envy within us, we ought to be aware of how expensive that envy is. The envious person is an unhappy person. In fact, he is doubly unhappy—unhappy over what he lacks and unhappy over what his neighbor possesses, unhappy over his own troubles and unhappy over his neighbor's triumphs. Envy can be expensive in other ways, too. When a very promising post-office official was arrested recently and charged with staging a million-dollar robbery in his own post office, a co-worker offered this explanation: "He always seemed to want more—no matter what he had, he seemed to want more."

A rabbi in the Talmud, the massive collection of Jewish law and lore, warned against another consequence of envy: "He who focuses his attention on that which is not his is denied what he seeks and loses what he already has."

For all the unkind things we have said about envy, it would only be fair to acknowledge that not all envy is destructive. If envy leads us to work hard, to improve our skills and our capabilities, if it leads us to strive more diligently, then envy can goad us on to progress. Far from being destructive, envy then becomes a stimulus to self-advancement.

And envy can be used creatively in another way. If it is directed at the virtues of another, it can be a constructive force for growth and development. If Korach had envied Moses' profound dedication, his boundless love for his people, his perseverance in the face of repeated setbacks—if Korach had set his mind on these things, he might have striven to acquire them. Korach's problem was that he wanted the rewards of virtue without being virtuous; he wanted the fruits of service without serving.

God has given us no quality that cannot be used for good. We can use even our envy to become better human beings and more faithful carriers of His image.

The Idols We Worship

Two seasoned sailors heard the chaplain preach on the Ten Commandments. When the sermon was over, one sailor muttered to his friend: "Well, at least I never made any graven images."

That sailor, like most of us, looked upon the worship of idols as an ancient practice, characteristic of primitive people. In fact, the second commandment has been called "the obsolete commandment." But is it? Has idolatry really disappeared in the twentieth century? Not if some of our most perceptive observers are to be believed. "Contemporary life," wrote philosopher Will Herberg, "is idolatry-ridden to an appalling degree."

In many of the cults that have proliferated in our time, idolatry has appeared in the blind, submissive worship of the guru, the infallible leader, the one who, through brainwashing, has gained even the power to command the believer to commit suicide at his behest. The tragedy of Jim Jones and the People's Temple in Guyana was the result of this insidious form of idolatry.

In his important book, *Crazy for God,* Christopher Edwards, a former Moonie, provides a glimpse into the nightmare of cult life and, in the process, reveals its idolatrous character. He shows us the Moonies swaying back and forth around a picture of the Reverend Moon, bowing down on command before the portrait, and praying to him as "our new Messiah, the Creator and giver of true life . . . Father, we pledge our lives to you, our hearts, our souls!"

We human beings are born believers. Believing is as natural to us as breathing. And nature abhors a spiritual vacuum. When we stop believing in God we do not believe in *nothing.* We believe in *anything.* When God departs, the little gods come rushing in, "and some dark spirit sitteth in His seat" (Robert Browning).

The brutal madness called Nazism dethroned God and replaced Him with a malicious idol. This grace was recited by small children in Nazi Germany: "Führer, my Führer, sent to me from God, protect and maintain me throughout my life. Thou who hast saved Germany from deepest need, I thank thee for my daily bread. Remain at my side and never leave me, Führer, my Führer, my faith, my light. Heil, my Führer."

The word *worship* is derived from an old English word meaning "worth." That which assumes supreme worth in our eyes, that is what we worship, that becomes our God. Understood in this light, it is not only cultists and Nazis who are idolaters.

We can and do make graven images of power, status, or wealth. On their altars we bring supreme sacrifices. To obtain them we often surrender our honor, compromise our character, neglect our families, destroy our health.

A recent cartoon shows two aristocratic-looking gentlemen sitting in heavily upholstered chairs. One says to the other: "It was terrible! I dreamed the dollar was no longer worth worshipping!"

It is only when we understand the powerful appeal of idolatry that we appreciate why a Jew is expected to repeat morning and evening, every day of his life: "Hear O Israel, the Lord our God, the Lord is One."

God alone is to be worshipped. To Him alone we are to dedicate all that we are and all that we possess.

A shoe manufacturer condensed this whole philosophy of life in a small sign that sat on his desk: "God first; shoes second."

Things God Cannot Do Without Us

One of the most thrilling passages in the Bible is the one with which it opens. It transports us to the very beginning of things, to the fresh dawn of creation when we hear the Divine voice summoning order out of chaos, light out of darkness, life out of the unchartered void. After six days of creation, we read, "And God saw everything that He had made, and behold it was very good" (Genesis 1:31). "Very good"—but not perfect.

A young man who was depressed by the evil, the suffering, the misery of the world complained to his rabbi: "Why did God ever make such a world? Why, I could make a better world than this myself." His rabbi answered quietly: "That is exactly the reason God put you in this world—to make it a better world. Now go ahead and do your part."

In the rabbi's answer, we come upon a subtle truth that is frequently overlooked. We always talk of our dependence upon God. We seem to forget that God also depends on us. There are so many things He cannot do without us. "Man," taught the ancient sages, is "a partner to the Holy One, blessed be He, in the work of creation." And, may I add, not a silent partner, either.

Now I don't know why God put us in an unfinished world. Perhaps life would have no purpose in a finished world. But here we are in a world crying to be made better, each with our own selves capable of becoming better and God asking us to do these jobs with Him because He cannot do them alone.

God cannot make a peaceful world unless we, His children, help Him by rooting out the hatred from our hearts, the prejudice from our minds, the injustice from our society.

God cannot build a happy home unless husband and wife work with Him by bringing to it a spirit of sharing, mutual respect, a binding loyalty, constancy, and compassion.

God cannot give us a peaceful night's sleep unless we cooperate with Him by doing an honest day's work.

God cannot forgive our sins unless we help Him by genuine

contrition for what has been and firm resolve for what we mean to accomplish.

God heals the sick but not without the surgeon's hands, the doctor's medicine, the nurse's vigilance, the encouragement of loved ones and friends.

God brings forth bread from the earth but not without the farmer who prepares the soil, plants the seed, harvests the crop.

God helps the poor with the charity we give, cheers the lonely with the visits we make, comforts the bereaved with the words we speak, guides our children with the examples we set, ennobles our lives with the good deeds we perform.

And here, ultimately, may be the reason that you and I are here on this earth. God needs us, each of us. We are joined with Him in a great partnership.

We Are Each Indispensable in Our Small Parts

If all people on earth have a set of common ancestors—Adam and Eve—and, therefore, a common point of origin, we would expect them all to be speaking a common language. How, then, does it happen that there is in fact a multiplicity of tongues in use throughout the world?

The Bible addresses itself to this unspoken question in the celebrated story of the misguided people who built the Tower of Babel. What was their goal? "Come let us build ourselves a city and a tower, with its top in Heaven, and let us make ourselves a name" (Genesis 11:4). They believed that if they built the tallest tower, a heaven-scraper, they would acquire instant fame. Instead, the Bible tells us, they were doubly punished. They suffered a confusion of languages wherein all they could do was babble unintelligibly, and they were scattered abroad on the face of the earth. What was their sin?

It was, I suspect, that they mistook bigness for greatness, quantity for quality, size for substance. This particular sin did not disappear with the tower builders; it is yet alive and well among us.

We live in a time addicted to bigness—bigger industries, bigger bombs, king-size cigarettes and giant movie screens. One Hollywood producer said that he wanted a film that began with an earthquake and worked up to a climax. In our concern with bigness, we have forgotten that a poor film becomes only more tedious by being prolonged and that a nation bent on enslaving others becomes only more dangerous as its power increases.

Greatness is a matter not of size but of quality; and it is within the reach of every one of us. Greatness lies in the faithful performance of whatever duties life places upon us and in the generous performance of the small acts of kindness that God has made possible for us. There is greatness in patient endurance; in unyielding loyalty to a goal; in resistance to the temptation to betray the best we know; in speaking up for the truth when it is assailed; in steadfast adherence to vows given and promises made.

God does not ask us to do extraordinary things. He asks us to do ordinary things extraordinarily well.

Let none of us believe that greatness has passed us by. If we wish it very much, it can be ours. Of each of us it can be said, as it was of an actor who had played minor roles for twenty-five years, "He was indispensable in small parts."

Each of us is indispensable in the part assigned to us by the Master Playwright. Each of us has a job to do that will remain undone if we do not do it. Each of us has love that only we can give. Each of us has compassion that will be denied to the world if we suppress it. We are each indispensable in our small parts and each part is gilded with a glory all its own.

Discovering Our Own Worth

The late Dorothy Parker was once at a cocktail party at which someone praised another prominent woman by saying, "She's very kind to her inferiors." Miss Parker then asked caustically, "And where does she find them?"

Stripped of its malice, the question points to a truth that applies to all of us. Where do we find our inferiors?

Indeed, isn't there something twisted in us when we begin to divide people into the categories of superior and inferior? Are we not obliged to consider other human beings simply as human beings and accord them the consideration and courtesy due them by virtue of this towering endowment?

This would seem to be the thrust of a comment that a Jewish teacher of old made on a rather undistinguished-looking segment of a biblical verse: "And the Lord said unto Moses: 'Speak unto the priests, the sons of Aaron, and speak unto them . . .' " (Leviticus 21:1). The ancient sage questioned the repetitious use of the verb *speak*. One "speak" would have been quite sufficient.

The purpose of the apparent redundancy, he said, was to caution the prominent people about how they shall speak to the humble people: "We warn the 'big' people not to speak disdainfully to the 'little' people."

This concern for the feelings and the dignity of the humblest of people has always been one of the hallmarks of Judaism. It derived its major nourishment from that magnificent and daring affirmation in the opening chapter of Genesis, that God created man in His own image.

Our human worth derives from our exalted Source. We each come from God, and we carry within us the divine imprint. "There is no great and no small to the Soul that maketh all."

Measured against the infinite greatness of God, how significant is the difference between the "biggest" and "smallest" of people?

We are told that Alexander the Great once found Diogenes carefully examining a parcel of human bones, and he asked the philosopher what he was looking for. "I am looking," replied Diogenes, "for that which I cannot find—the difference between your father's bones and those of his slaves."

One year, on the eve of the new year, a New York newspaper asked some prominent citizens what they would like to see accomplished during the coming year in their city. An actress gave the following answer: "Well, if I had a magic wand, I would like everyone to be able to feel that they really counted. There seems to be a sense of impotence today, and it would be great if everyone really knew that they were important in a very real sense."

We are each important in a very real sense, and it is a great day for us when we discover that sense of self worth. When we learn to respect ourselves, it becomes easier to respect others. And then we do not need to feel superior to anyone. We are just glad to be ourselves.

Predicting the Future

The future has been defined as something everyone reaches at the rate of sixty minutes an hour, whatever he does, whoever he is. But there has always been a vast curiosity to know the future before we get there.

Every day, some 50 million Americans read that special section in 1,200 newspapers to learn what the planets have in store for them. Astrology is a busy occupation in America today. Ten thousand people are working at it full time and another 175,000 part time.

We consult the stars, the tea leaves, the palm readers, the crystal balls, in an effort to part the curtain that veils the future. A recent cartoon shows a young girl reading her diary to a friend, and she says: "This is one book where I wish it were possible to peek in the back and see how it comes out."

Even the biblical patriarch Jacob attempted for a fleeting moment to unravel the secrets that are hidden in the womb of time. As he lay upon his deathbed, he gathered his children and said to them: "Come together that I may tell you what is to befall you in days to come" (Genesis 49:1).

As we read further, however, there are no predictions of things to come. And our sages pointed out that "Jacob wanted to foretell the future, but the Divine presence departed from him." God apparently did not want the future to be revealed. Why not?

If you and I knew what was going to happen tomorrow and the day after and on all the tomorrows that are to be, wouldn't life lose its zest and its excitement? Wouldn't a terrible boredom set in as we played out mechanically the roles that had been predetermined for us?

And if we knew in advance all the heartbreak and the disappointments, the blasted hopes and the broken dreams, the small sorrows and the inconsolable griefs that awaited us—could we find the courage to venture into the future at all?

But the most compelling reason no one can predict the future is that the future does not exist. You and I are not robots. We have freedom of will to determine the shape of tomorrow by what we do today.

James Truslow Adams, the American historian, put his finger on the truth when he said that while an astronomer can predict precisely where every star will be at 11:30 tonight, he can make no such prediction about his young daughter.

What the future has in store for us depends largely on what we place in store for the future. Not the stars, nor the cards, but our own actions will determine the shape of things to come.

The Fine Art of Discrimination

To members of a minority group, *discrimination* is a fighting word. It conjures up quotas, "gentlemen's agreements," economic barriers, "exclusive" country clubs and hotels. Discrimination can be a dangerous social disease. As one of its frequent victims, a Jew knows only too well the injustice and the pain discrimination inflicts.

And yet, the Bible repeatedly calls upon us to exercise the fine art of discrimination. We are urged to discriminate between the sacred and the profane, between the clean and the unclean (Leviticus 10:10, 11:47). Thus the Bible reminds us that the capacity to discriminate, to distinguish, is one of the most precious human endowments.

As a matter of fact, discrimination is something we have to practice every hour of every day of our lives. We have to be discriminating in our choice of activities, in the pursuits in which we are going to invest our time.

In his later years, Joseph Conrad, author of the great novel *Heart of Darkness,* wrote, "I remember my youth and the feeling that I could last forever, outlast the sea, the earth and all men." As we grow older, we realize, of course, that we do not last forever. We do not have unlimited time at our disposal. The man with limited funds cannot buy everything in the Sears Roebuck catalogue. With limited time we cannot do everything, either. If we are going to invest our time wisely, we need a fine sense of discrimination.

If we were told that we had thirty days to live, how would we choose to spend those days? How many of the things that we are not doing now would we start doing in a mighty hurry? How many of the things that we are doing now would we stop doing rather promptly? "There is no time for all things," said Shakespeare.

Our minds cannot harbor all thoughts. If we clutter them up with prejudices and hatreds, with pettiness and poisoned memories, we are abusing a delicate and precious instrument. The art of discrimination involves great care in the choice of thoughts to which we grant a seat in the arena of our minds.

Elizabeth Peabody was one of the pioneers in the kindergarten movement in our country. When she began her school, she advertised that it would be a "very exclusive school." And indeed it was—most exclusive. It was exclusive in the highest sense of the word. As she explained it, "snobbery and vulgarity are vigorously excluded." We all need a lot more of that exclusiveness, for this is the art of discrimination at its highest.

At Life's Moral Crossroads Proceed with Caution

A motorist in a strange city came to a busy intersection and could not decide how to proceed. The traffic lights turned from red to green to amber three times while he tried to make up his mind. At last the traffic policeman came over to him and asked, "What's the matter, bud, don't we have a color you like?"

As a driver who regularly gets lost trying to reach Pennsauken, New Jersey, from Philadelphia—a distance of only a few miles—my sympathies are all with our indecisive motorist. But I wonder whether his dilemma is not a parable of a problem that affects vast numbers of people in our time. We find ourselves repeatedly at moral and ethical crossroads, and we have lost our sense of direction. We are not sure which way to go. Should we stop? Proceed with caution? Go straight ahead? Turn off the road altogether?

It is not easy to make moral decisions these days. Moral values have become blurred. Old standards of behavior once taken for granted are being widely challenged and openly flouted. Time-honored institutions are being disregarded. In the words of Marc Connelly, the popular playwright: "Everything nailed down is coming loose." How then does one proceed in an age of uncertain guideposts and disappearing landmarks?

If we are unable or unwilling to accept the ancient "thou shalts" and "thou shalt nots," then perhaps the following questions can help us make our moral decisions.

First question: Can the decision I make stand the glare of publicity? What if everybody knew about it? Does it need a cover-up? Could I tell my mother or my son what I did?

"It is an awful hour," wrote a wise counselor, "when the first necessity of hiding anything comes. . . . When there are questions to be feared and eyes to be avoided and subjects which must not be touched, then the bloom of life is gone. Put off that day as long as possible. Put it off forever if you can."

Second question: Will my best self approve the action I am contemplating? Does it satisfy my own highest standards of behavior? Is it compatible with my conscience? Will it leave me with guilt or with pride?

Third question: Where does this action lead to? What are its likely results? Long ago a Jewish sage asked, "Who is wise?" and answered, "He who sees the consequences of his deed." A clever man tries to get out of a mess a wise man wouldn't have gotten into in the first place.

Last question: What if everybody did what I am contemplating, what kind of society would we fashion? Would the world be a better or a shabbier place to live in if my action became the accepted norm, the universal guide?

We sometimes try to maintain our moral neutrality by saying that there are two sides to every question. True enough, and there are two sides to a sheet of flypaper, but it makes a big difference to the fly which side he chooses.

In *The Moral Decision,* Edmond Cahn, the American jurist, reminded us how much depends on the decisions each of us makes: "When any human being, however obscure, decides to follow the more benevolent of the courses presented before him, the dynamic good in his choice explodes and penetrates through all the communities of men."

At life's moral crossroads, let us proceed with caution. We are being followed.

Everything in Moderation?

Two friends who had not seen each other for some time were engaged in an animated discussion when one of them asked, "Would you want me to read your horoscope?"

"I didn't know you believe in astrology," her friend replied.

"Oh," said the first friend, "I believe in everything a little bit."

Many of us are that way—we believe in many things a little bit. We hedge our spiritual bets. We are reluctant to make total commitments. We don't mind too much being classified as "religious" but we would not want to be considered "fanatics." Everything in moderation.

Sidney Lanier, the nineteenth-century American poet and critic, captured the mood of our time when he wrote:

> *We live in an age of half faith and half doubt;*
> *Standing at the Temple doors head in, heart out.*

To those of us who share the spiritual ambivalence of our time, there is a well-known biblical verse that ought to shake us up: "You must love the Lord your God with all your heart and with all your soul and with all your might" (Deuteronomy 6:5). The Scriptures ask us to love God totally, completely, with our whole being. Moderation is not enough.

Indeed, as we stop to think about it, we realize that the statement "Everything in moderation" is only moderately true.

In studying the credentials of a prospective employee, a bank executive would not be overly impressed by a letter of recommendation describing the applicant as being "moderately honest." A defendant on trial for his life would not choose a lawyer who was moderately competent. A parent with a desperately ill child would not choose a doctor who is moderately skillful. And there is not too much hope for a marriage in which the partners are moderately faithful. When a man is drowning twenty feet offshore, a fifteen-foot-long rope will not do. In certain crucial areas, moderation is simply not enough.

The love of God is one of these areas. Every morning and every evening, the Jew recites the words found in the mezuzah, the small traditional ornamental container that Jews affix to their doorframes: "You must love the Lord your God with *all* your heart and with *all* your soul and with *all* your might."

Make Warm Fuzzies—Today

"What did you do in school today?" I asked six-year-old Daniella.

"We made warm fuzzies."

"Warm fuzzies? What are warm fuzzies?"

"Well," she said slowly, trying to find words that even a grandfather could understand, "warm fuzzies are things that you say that make people feel good." And then, reaching into her schoolbag, she added, "Here are some of the warm fuzzies I got."

"You ar my best frend."

"You are veeree prittee."

"Yu I lik."

"I liek the prezint you gave mee."

Much later that evening I thought of the lesson Daniella's teacher had taught her class. How much easier life would be for all of us if we concentrated on handing out warm fuzzies to the people whose lives intersect our own in the course of any day. Mark Twain once said that he could live on a good compliment for two months. How long has it been since we gave a warm fuzzy to our children, our mates, the people who serve us, our brothers and sisters?

On the occasion of his ninety-fourth birthday, the late Will Durant was interviewed by the press. One of our most prolific authors, he wrote, with his wife, Ariel, an eleven-volume biography of mankind, *The Story of Civilization*. In the interview, Durant was asked what piece of wisdom he would distill from a lifetime of reading and reflecting. "If you insist upon one brief answer," he said, "I say kindness. And that is, in my opinion, the finest, most successful method of behavior, not merely of a man to his wife, or vice versa, but of a man to his neighbor, of any individual to the individuals he meets."

Daniella says warm fuzzies. Durant says kindness.

How desperate is our need for kindness! So many of us hunger for it most of the time. One doctor has estimated that 90 percent of all the mental illness he has treated could have been prevented or cured by ordinary kindness. What an indictment against us! All

46

around us there is emotional starvation, and we do not have the time or the thoughtfulness or the compassion to speak a kind word, perform a gracious act, pay a visit, drop a line, make a warm fuzzy.

Kindness is a universal language which even an animal can understand and even the mute can speak. The person who has not learned kindness remains uneducated no matter how many diplomas adorn his office walls or the number of degrees that follow his signature. The person who has learned to be kind has mastered the most vital subject in life's curriculum. His formal schooling may be meager, his familiarity with books not very intimate. If he has learned how to bring a ray of light where there is darkness, a touch of softness where life has been hard, a word of cheer to lift drooping spirits—that person is best equipped to live life as it should be lived.

In *The Summing Up,* W. Somerset Maugham tries to communicate the essence of what he learned in all his years. He too comes to the conclusion that the most important thing in life is kindness. And then he hastens to add that he is ashamed that he has reached so commonplace a conclusion. He would have liked to leave his readers with some sort of startling revelation or with a glittering epigram of sparkling originality. "It seems," he says ruefully, "I have little more to say than can be read in any copybook or heard from any pulpit. I have gone a long way round to discover what everyone knew already."

Daniella is learning the lesson early. Make warm fuzzies—today.

Your Pain in My Heart

One of the most sublime summaries of the essence of religion is found in one of the shortest books in the Bible.

Almost 2,700 years ago, the prophet Micah told his contemporaries "what is good and what the Lord requires of you: to act justly, to love mercy, and to walk humbly with your God" (Micah 6:8).

Each of the three virtues Micah underscores—justice, mercy, and humility—is deserving of extended comment. But now I would like to zero in on the middle one—mercy. The Hebrew word that we translate here as "mercy" is *chesed*. Judaism did not permit mercy to remain merely a feeling, a kind of inner glow of benevolence or pity. It demanded that that feeling be translated into a host of benevolent acts. Such an act is called *gemilut chesed,* an act of loving-kindness.

Here are some of those acts: visiting the sick, comforting the bereaved, extending hospitality to strangers, caring for the orphan and the widow, promoting peace between people.

The rabbis pointed out the distinction between giving charity and performing an act of loving-kindness. Charity involves financial help, while an act of loving-kindness can be performed with money or with one's person. Charity is given only to the poor, but an act of loving-kindness can be shown to the rich as well as to the poor. Charity is extended only to the living, while an act of loving-kindness can be conferred even upon the dead.

An act of loving-kindness is a humane response to human need. It is your pain in my heart.

Loving-kindness reveals the inability to remain content in the presence of a person who is troubled; the inability to remain comfortable in the presence of a person who is uncomfortable; the inability to enjoy serenity when one's neighbor is distressed.

The most important art to be cultivated in life is the art of loving-kindness. The person who has mastered it is doing God's work here on earth.

The ultimate tribute to loving-kindness is found in this rabbinic passage:

There are ten strong things. Iron is strong, but fire melts it. Fire is strong, but water quenches it. Water is strong, but the clouds evaporate it. Clouds are strong, but wind drives them away. Man is strong, but fear casts him down. Fear is strong, but wine allays it. Wine is strong, but sleep overcomes it. Sleep is strong, but death is stronger, and loving-kindness survives death.

The Gifts We Do Not Give

Prophets are said to be without honor in their own country—and even Moses was no exception to this melancholy rule. His contemporaries tried to cut him down to size.

They complained to him, gossiped about him, maligned him, and the opposition led by Korach rebelled against him.

The ancient Jewish sages pictured Korach trying to discredit Moses by mocking his teachings.

"You have taught us," Korach argued, " 'Do not rob the poor for he is poor' " (Proverbs 22:22). "Ridiculous! How can one possibly rob the poor? Since he is poor there is nothing to rob from him."

Moses replied, "The charity you should give to the poor belongs to him. When you fail to give it to him, you are robbing him!"

A subtle, sensitive truth speaks to us here. Robbing does not always involve taking from another; sometimes we rob by failing to give what belongs to us. We impoverish others by the gifts we withhold from them, by the support we deny them.

And it is not only material things we are talking about. Some of the most treasured gifts we persistently fail to offer cannot be bought or sold.

Who among us is so poor he has no kindness to give? Who is so rich he does not need it?

Recently a boy ran afoul of the law, and his father was called to the police station. In the course of the pained conversation that followed, the boy absorbed his father's stern rebuke, then spoke with mature insight:

"The problem is you never listen to me. You're too busy making money to give me things. I don't need your money. I need you."

Another illustration of our theme is found in *The Fool,* a play by Channing Pollock. In one scene, a woman speaks of her furs as "a substitute for my husband's time and love and companionship."

The husband's father reacts to this remark: "I don't know what you women want. A man works his heart and soul out to get you things and still you are not satisfied."

The wife replies, "Maybe we would like a little heart and soul."

What extravagant gifts are ours to bestow! A word of praise so many yearn to hear, encouragement to lighten the burden of living, an hour to listen to a loved one's heart, an act of forgiveness to repair a family breach, a thoughtful deed to brighten a dreary day—these gifts we too often withhold are so desperately needed and so amply at our disposal.

As we bestow these gifts on others, they come back to enrich our lives.

Do not rob the poor because . . . you may be robbing yourself.

Giving and Living

A candidate for the police force was asked what he would do to disperse a threatening mob. He thought for a while, then answered with a look of self-satisfaction, "I'd start to take up a collection."

The young man understood human psychology. We resist giving, and an appeal for funds can send us scurrying for shelter. But here, as in so many other areas of life, what we seek strenuously to evade is what we should diligently strive to embrace.

Many of us are familiar with the exhortation " 'Tis better to give than to receive." A profounder truth is that in the very act of giving, we are receiving. As we give, we live.

This truth is built into the very structure of a Hebrew word that is used in conjunction with one of the very earliest biblical references to making financial contributions. In the Book of Exodus (30:12) we read that when Moses wanted to take a census of the male adult Israelites, they were each to give a half-shekel, and Moses was then to count the coins. The English words "and they shall give" are expressed in Hebrew in a single word: *ve-natnu*. Now, the striking feature of that word is that in Hebrew it is a palindrome: It reads the same in both directions. Thus, it seems to be telling us that what we give comes right back to us. The act of giving is simultaneously an act of receiving. The benefactor is also the beneficiary. To give is to become enriched.

Our truth springs not so much from the structure of a Hebrew word as it does from the structure of the human being. God so fashioned us that we are not satisfied merely to be satisfied. We have a deep-rooted craving to give satisfaction.

Erich Fromm, the noted psychologist, has underlined this truth: "Not he who has much is rich, but he who gives much. The hoarder, who is anxiously worried about losing something, is, psychologically speaking, the poor impoverished man, regardless of how much he has. Whoever is capable of giving of himself is rich."

As we feed, we are fed. As we give, we receive. As we lift, we are raised. As we go out of ourselves into something bigger than ourselves, we become bigger in the process and we provide the most nourishing sustenance our craving hearts demand.

"Help your brother's boat across, and lo, your own has reached the shore."

Listening with the Heart

In a recent cartoon, our pathetic but lovable friend Ziggy passes a rather shabby-looking character who is sitting on the sidewalk propped up against a building. Beside him there is a sign that announces: "Good Listener—25 cents for 5 minutes."

The sidewalk solicitor had greatly underpriced his services, for we happen to be suffering from a terrible shortage of good listeners. Like the biblical woman of valor, a good listener's worth "is far above rubies."

Almost any day the classified sections of our newspapers announce courses and seminars that promise to make us better speakers. But where are the courses to make us better listeners? Among the prizes awarded at commencement exercises there is usually one for the graduate who has shown excellence in public speaking. But did you ever hear of a prize awarded to a student for excellence in private listening?

When a prominent TV personality decided to quit a popular network program, he gave this explanation for his surprising action: "I've become increasingly aware of late that for the past ten years I've been on the air doing a great deal of talking. I want to start looking, thinking, and listening to people."

Anatomically speaking, you and I are so constructed that we should devote more time to listening than to speaking. The Divine Architect endowed us with two ears but only one mouth. Yet for most of us the mouth is a sorely overworked organ and the ears are in a state of semiretirement.

A bartender who was breaking in a young apprentice saw the novice hard at work trying to be witty and humorous with the customers. Unhappily, he wasn't making much of an impression. Finally, the veteran called the young man aside and gave him the distilled wisdom of years of experience: "Listen, kid, listen. Don't talk. These guys want to talk. If they wanted to listen, they'd go home."

That veteran bartender knew a lot more than how to mix a drink. He was a keen student of human nature. He understood how desperately we each need someone who will listen to us, someone to whom we can speak of our fears and our frustrations, our loneliness and our despair, our angers and our anxieties, our defeats and our disappointments; someone to whom we can recount our occasional triumphs and our self-enhancing accomplishments. We each need someone to release us from the isolation cell to which we are so frequently consigned because no one cares enough to liberate us by the simple act of listening.

A good listener is worth considerably more than twenty-five cents for five minutes. Psychiatrists' offices are crowded with people willing to pay substantial fees to satisfy their hunger to be heard. Many a family breakup is directly traceable to a failure in communication. There's a great deal of talking and even shouting, but very little listening.

One family therapist who has achieved much success in his work explains his method: "I really don't do much of anything to get families together. I simply give each member a chance to talk while the others listen—without interrupting. Often it's the first time they've listened to each other in years."

His words have the sharp sting of recognition. The next time we are sorely tempted to give our children a "talking to," let us first pause to ask ourselves when the last time was we gave them a "listening to." And this goes for husbands and wives too.

Listening is not easy. If it were, there wouldn't be such a shortage in that department. Listening to another, really listening with our whole person, requires discipline, patience, and, above all, lots of caring. But how great are the rewards of listening. Through creative listening we exercise the magic that makes the other person feel so very important, and at the same time we ourselves break out of our own isolation. We open channels of communication that enable us to touch and be touched, to expand others while we ourselves are enlarged.

When God appeared to King Solomon in a vision in the night and offered him any gift he wished, the wise monarch asked for neither power nor wealth, nor glory. He asked instead for "a listening heart." It is a gift worth cultivating. For, ultimately, true listening is not done with the ears. It is done with the heart.

No Appreciation Without Reciprocation

In one of his letters, Robert Southey, the nineteenth-century English poet, tells of a Spaniard who "always put on his spectacles when he was about to eat strawberries so that they might look bigger and more tempting. In just the same way," adds Southey, "I make the most of my enjoyments."

These are words worth pondering. If only we could learn to magnify our blessings instead of exaggerating our troubles! Most of the time we are putting on our spectacles when we look at the things we lack. How large they loom. How we permit them to rankle. How often we permit the fly in the ointment to grow so huge that we see only the fly and forget that we also possess the ointment.

Grandma's eyesight wasn't as good as it used to be, but there was nothing wrong with her perspective. When asked about her health, she answered softly: "I have two teeth left and thank God they are directly opposite one another." Her spectacles were properly focused.

A true perspective on our possessions also serves to remind us that they are given to us in trust, to use not only for our own pleasures and gratification but also in the service of others. Gratitude at its highest goes beyond *saying* thanks to *giving* thanks. We are not truly grateful until we make it possible for others to experience gratitude too.

This, after all, is what we really mean when we say "much obliged." We mean that we are much obligated, we have incurred a debt which we are duty bound to repay. What is involved is not generosity but common honesty.

Every blessing we enjoy has been sacrificially paid for by others. Our freedom, our health, our heritage, our security, are all dipped in the blood of generations of benefactors. Such obligations can never be fully liquidated. But neither are we exempt from making some sustained effort at repayment.

If we are truly thankful for our freedom, we must be vitally concerned with the plight of those who still wear chains. If we are grateful for our share of God's abundance, we must share that abundance with the ill-fed, the ill-clad, the ill-housed. "There is no lovelier way to thank God for your sight," wrote Helen Keller, "than by giving a helping hand to someone in the dark."

No appreciation without reciprocation.

An oft-repeated prayer asks:

> *You have given so much to me,*
> *Give me one thing more—a grateful heart.*

And, we might add, a generous hand.

The Big Role of Little Things

The last page I read to her before tucking her in for the night had the old favorite that begins with the lines: "For want of a nail, the shoe was lost. For want of a shoe, the horse was lost . . ." and so on. The loss of the horse led to the loss of the rider, the battle, and, finally, the kingdom itself. All for want of a nail.

After she had fallen asleep, I wondered whether her five-year-old mind had grasped the profound meaning of the simple poem. Its message is meant for people of all ages: Pay large attention to the little things.

A tragic illustration of the crucial importance of little things was furnished a few years ago by the crash of a jet airliner shortly after takeoff. All ninety-five persons aboard were killed. An exhaustive study of the disaster concluded that it might have been caused by the loss in the rudder-control system of a little bolt, less than an inch long. For want of a bolt, so many lives were lost.

Little things have not only been responsible for huge losses, they have also triggered great discoveries. A spider web over a garden path led to the suspension bridge. A teakettle singing on the stove was the inspiration for the steam engine. A falling apple suggested the law of gravity. A lantern swinging in a tower was responsible for the pendulum.

On both sides of the historical ledger, great consequences have come from little things.

In our personal lives, too, little things play a far greater role than we usually realize. Little things give us pain, and little things give us pleasure. A cruel word can cast a dreary cloud over the brightest of days; a word of appreciation can send our spirits soaring. A small act of kindness can often make a big difference in the delicate machinery of the human spirit.

When the English writer Oscar Wilde was being led handcuffed from prison to the Court of Bankruptcy, a friend waited for him to pass through the dreary, drafty corridor. As the prisoner passed, his friend tipped his hat to him. Of this gesture Wilde wrote later, "The memory of this little, lovely, silent act of love has unsealed for me all the wells of pity."

Few of us are ever asked to do great things, but we are always given the opportunity to do little things in a great way. Some of the most heroic people I have known have been anonymous little people who inspired me by the spectacular way they performed ordinary, unspectacular deeds.

I have known parents who have cared for a handicapped child day after day, week after week, year after year, compensating for nature's frail endowments with double portions of inexhaustible love. I have known young widows who have managed for long years to be both mother and father to their children. I have known humble people who have a boundless capacity for bringing cheer into lonely lives, who are drawn by some special instinct to human need, who are always scrubbing the little corner assigned to them to make it brighter and cleaner.

Perhaps Rabbi Leo Baeck summed up our theme best: "Piety . . . respects the little—the little man, the little task, the little duty. Through the little, religion meets the greatness that lies behind."

An Eternity Case

The obstretrician was not at home. His five-year-old daughter answered the doorbell. "Is your daddy in?" asked an excited stranger. "No, he's gone," the little girl replied. "When will he return?" "I don't know. He's out on an eternity case."

The little girl was right. Every child is an eternity case—the heir of all that has gone before, the molder of all that is to be.

The birth of a child is such a commonplace thing. It happens about 100,000 times a day. And yet each child is born just once. Each child is an original, altogether unique and so enormously special. Each is a miracle, a tiny bundle of infinite possibilities, mysterious and unpredictable. Do we know—can we possibly imagine—what secret that child carries, what hidden splendor that tiny frame embodies?

Dr. E. T. Sullivan, an American clergyman, has alerted us to the tremendous difference a single child can make. He points out that when God wants a great work done in the world or a great wrong righted, he doesn't stir up earthquakes or send forth thunderbolts. Instead, a baby is born. God then puts the idea into the mother's heart, and she puts it into the baby's mind. And then God waits. The greatest forces in the world are not earthquakes and thunderbolts. The greatest forces in the world are babies.

How can we be certain that the newborn child will fulfill his or her promise? How can parents bring out the specialness, the uniqueness each child represents? There are no sure answers to any of these questions. There are no certainties and there are many risks where children are concerned. There are so many ways for young people to go astray, and there are a hundred ways they can break their parents' hearts.

"But a child is far less likely to get into trouble," writes Ardis Whitman, "if his mother and father find delight in living with him, if they are brave enough to hold him to the standards of performance we call discipline, and if they can take him as they take themselves—frail and full of faults, but moved now and then by a dream so big there are no words for it."

No Two Children Are Alike

"Horse sense" has been defined as that sense in a horse that keeps him from betting on a man. This definition may contain a touch of cynicism, but it also has a huge kernel of truth. Human beings are full of surprises, and human actions are frustratingly unpredictable.

Perhaps this is not the major point of the biblical story of the rivalry between the twin brothers Jacob and Esau, but it is surely a legitimate lesson to be derived from it. They emerge from the same womb, are nurtured in the same home, reared by the same parents—and yet how strikingly different they are in temperament, in outlook, in their life's values.

Esau is the rugged outdoor type, a physical person, athletic, sensuous, self-indulgent. Jacob is turned inward, sensitive to things of the mind and things of the spirit, preferring the quiet, reflective, studious life. So close together at birth, so far apart in their unfolding.

The diverging destinies of the twin brothers is mirrored in a remarkable phenomenon in nature. At one point in the Rocky Mountains, ten thousand feet above sea level, there are two streams of water that run in opposite directions. One of them moves toward the east and ultimately empties into the Gulf of Mexico. The other stream flows toward the west and finally empties into the Pacific Ocean.

How close these two streams were at their beginning, but how far apart they are at the end!

What is the point of all this? The point is that each child is unique, and yet, with all the best intentions and the most devoted care, parents can accomplish only so much with a child. Parents ought not to punish themselves too severely when, having done their best, things do not turn out the way they had hoped. Parents should also recognize inherent limitations, not only in what they can do but also in what they may do.

There was a time when the behavioral psychologists convinced us that the newborn child is like a blank sheet of paper waiting for the parents to write on it. Today we know better.

The child comes into the world with its basic temperament determined by the accidental combination of genes that carry not only the traits of its parents, but also of ancestors long forgotten. And no two children are alike. That is why one authority tells us that bringing up children by the book is well enough, provided we remember that we need a different book for each child.

In his epic poem *Hermann and Dorothea,* Goethe puts the following words into the mouth of the wise mother:

We have no power to fashion our children as suits our fancy;
As they are given by God, so must we have them and love them;
Teach them as best we can, and let each of them follow his nature.
One will have talents of one sort, and different talents another.
Every one uses his own, in his own individual fashion.

Time—the Thoughtful Thief

Is time an ally or an antagonist? It depends. It depends on how we look upon time and how we use it.

Time has been called a thief. There is much truth in that designation. Time robs us of our loved ones, steals the spring from our steps, the bloom from our cheeks, the smoothness from our skins.

But, if time is a thief, it is not without a core of compassion. For everything it takes, it thoughtfully leaves something behind.

In place of loved ones, it leaves undying and enduring lessons. The bloom it stole, time replaced with lines it gently etched in bright moments of shared laughter and somber moments of chastening sorrow. If we can no longer run as quickly as we did yesterday, we can stand today with greater poise. And while time was stealing the smoothness from our skins, it was giving us the opportunity to remove the wrinkles from our souls.

Time does something else, too. Time converts knowledge into wisdom, energies spent into experience gained. Time leaves us richer for what we have had.

And time thoughtfully permits us to use the fire of youth to drive the engines of age. We can be young and old at the same time.

We can be young enough to believe in people, but old enough not to expect more from them than we are prepared to give.

We can be young enough to enjoy pleasure, but old enough to know that we miss the whole point of living if pleasure is all we pursue.

We can be young enough to acquire a new idea, and old enough to surrender an ancient prejudice.

We can be young enough to strive for success, but old enough to treasure the things that money cannot buy.

We can be young enough to wait to be attractive, but old enough to appreciate the beauty that is manufactured inside ourselves.

We can be young enough to seek companionship, but old enough to appreciate solitude.

We can be young enough to crave happiness, but old enough to know that the harvest of happiness is usually reaped by the hands of helpfulness.

We can be young enough to want to be loved, but old enough to strive to be lovable.

We can be young enough to pray as if everything depended on God, but old enough to act as if everything depended on us.

Growing Older Serenely

The coming of a new year is a time for mixed feelings. On one hand, we are grateful that we are still around to welcome it. But then again, the new year is a sharp reminder of the irreversible passage of the years, and as we grow older they seem to be passing much faster than they used to.

This awareness fills us with a certain amount of anxiety.

One of the most widespread fears we have is the fear of growing old. There are many symptoms of this fear. Cosmetics are, today, a multibillion-dollar industry. The billboards and daily newspapers carry ads that make old age appear not as a stage of life but as a betrayal of it.

William Lyon Phelps, the American teacher and essayist, once wrote about the alarm with which we greet the first gray hair. He went on to say:

> Now, one really ought not to be alarmed when one's hair turns gray; if it turned green or blue, then one ought to see a doctor. But when it turns gray that simply means that there is so much gray matter in the skull that there is no longer room for it; it comes out and discolors the hair.
>
> Don't be ashamed of your gray hair, wear it proudly like a flag. You are fortunate in a world of so many vicissitudes, to have lived long enough to earn it.

Now, one does not necessarily have to share Dr. Phelps's affection for gray hair. If we happen to prefer another color, we have a choice today, and if another color makes us more cheerful, we are each entitled to our personal preference.

But Dr. Phelps is entirely correct in sounding the caution against allowing the advancing years to plant the seeds of fear in our hearts. There has been monotonous repetition and widespread acceptance of the erroneous conception that life reaches its climax in youth.

Consider what it would really mean if it were true that youth is the happiest time of life. If that were so, then nothing would be sadder than a young person of twenty-five, for here would be someone who had reached the very peak of existence, the absolute height, and now could expect only decay, deterioration, and decline. This would be the greatest insult to human personality and human potential.

If we are to face the advancing years with serenity and hope, we must realize that God has arranged human life on an ascending scale, and that every age has its unique satisfactions and joys, just as every hour of the day has its own charm and loveliness.

True, old age is physical autumn, but it can be a spiritual springtime. This is probably what George Santayana had in mind when he said: "Never have I enjoyed youth so thoroughly as I have in my old age."

Age usually mellows wisdom, softens sorrows, bridles passions. It often brings peace to troubled spirits. At life's sunset, the storms have spent their violence, greed and ambition have released their grip. And in spite of the popular misconception, the later years are not without their creative powers.

Oliver Wendell Holmes once said, "If you haven't cut your name on the door by the time you've reached forty, you might as well put up your jack-knife." But the same Holmes didn't write *Over the Teacups* until he was seventy-five. Goethe completed *Faust* at eighty. Titian painted his historic masterpiece, *The Battle of Lepanto,* at ninety-eight. Henrietta Szold's remarkable work of rescuing children from the Nazi inferno did not begin until she was in her seventies, and Chaim Weizmann became the first president of Israel in his middle seventies.

A kindly lady who was asked by a child whether she was young or old, answered, "My dear, I have been young a very long time." Robert Browning's well-known lines give us hopeful expectation as we look ahead to the years to come:

> *Grow old along with me!*
> *The best is yet to be,*
> *The last of life, for which the first was made . . .*
> *Trust God: see all,*
> *Nor be afraid.*

Time—Friend or Foe?

One of the most common reactions to the beginning of a new year is a comment on the speed with which the last one blew past us.

"My," we say, "how quickly the year went by! Everything travels by jet these days, even time." If the last year has flown by for you, be grateful. It's an indication that the year has dealt gently with you.

The last year has not hurried by for all. For those who suffered months of pain, it has been a long year. For those who lost someone dear, it has been a long year. For those who paced hospital corridors, who waited for a loved one to return, who looked in vain for employment—for them time did not fly: It dragged by on heavy feet. When you're alone and lonely and your heart is aching for what you know will never be again, a single night can be endless.

But whether the last year flew by or crawled by, it has been ours. It has been woven into the fabric of our being. It is part of the immortal record. A new year has just dawned. How shall we greet it? Is time friend or foe? Ziggy, our friend on the comics page, believes that "God invented time to keep all our bills from happening at once."

Time is a great healer but a poor beautician. Time is a tailor specializing in alterations. Some changes are for the worse, some for the better. Actually, time is neither an ally nor an enemy. It is what we do with time that matters.

Time is mechanical. It moves irresistibly. We can neither accelerate it nor halt it nor reverse it.

In her most celebrated poem, "Rock Me to Sleep," Elizabeth Akers Allen expressed a genuine human wish when she wrote:

Backward, turn backward, O Time, in your flight,
Make me a child again just for tonight.

But neither for her nor for us will time turn backward. Only the TV camera permits replays. The film of life cannot be rewound.

Horace Mann, the great American educator, once put this announcement in a newspaper's lost-and-found column: "Lost somewhere between sunrise and sunset, two golden hours, each set with 60 diamond minutes. No reward is offered, for they are gone forever."

What can we do with time? Many things. We can kill it. We can waste it. The speeding motorist makes time. The prisoner does time. The idler passes time.

There is something else we can do with time. We can sanctify it. Certain days have been set aside as holy days.

How does time become holy? It becomes holy when we use it for holy purposes. Every religion sets aside such holy days. For the Jews the most important of these are the High Holy Days. They are a time to be reminded of the preciousness of every moment. They are a time to pause, to evaluate, to resolve; a time to forgive and to ask forgiveness; a time to remember things forgotten and to forget things too long remembered; a time to reclaim sacred things abandoned and to abandon unworthy things too highly cherished; a time to ask, "How are we using time?" Yes, time flies, but we are the navigators. More important than counting time is making time count.

There is a special urgency to the prayer of the Psalmist: "So teach us to count our days, that we may acquire a heart of wisdom."

Things That Cannot Be Hurried

A candidate for the police force was asked this question: "If you were alone in a police car and were pursued by a gang of desperate criminals in another car doing sixty miles an hour along a lonely road, what would you do?"

Without a moment's hesitation the candidate replied: "Seventy."

He was a natural child of the times. We tend to regard greater speed as the solution to almost all of life's problems, forgetting that there are so many things in life that cannot be hurried.

This is a lesson urgently needed by us of the "now" generation who want what we want when we want it. Even in the age of the jet plane, the computer, and instant coffee, there are many precious things that cannot be hurried.

The healing that follows bereavement cannot be hurried. The cultivation of a mature faith in God and a genuine understanding of life cannot be hurried.

The seed that strains to become an oak; the acquaintance that deepens into friendship and blossoms into love; the mind that seeks to accumulate the precious wisdom stored up by those who have gone before; the child who must be molded into a "mensch" (a civilized human being)—these are some of the things that cannot be hurried.

A surgeon about to begin an emergency operation cautioned his assistants: "Let's not hurry; we don't have a moment to lose."

A wise old adage reminds us that "Heaven cannot be gained by hurrying, and hell can wait." We would therefore do well to repeat regularly a prayer written by O. L. Crain:

Remind me each day that the race is not always to the swift and that there is more to life than increasing its speed. . . . Slow me down, God, and inspire me to send my roots deep into the soil of life's enduring values, that I may grow toward the stars of my greater destiny.

Golden Calf or Tabernacle?

Two biblical incidents in close proximity and in stark contrast to each other point up an important truth about ourselves and the things we own.

The first incident involved the fashioning of the golden calf. The Israelites who had so recently stood at Mount Sinai now suffer a moral relapse. When Moses delays his descent from the mountain, the ex-slaves panic, fashion a calf from their gold earrings, and proclaim: "This is your god, O Israel, who brought you out of the land of Egypt" (Exodus 32:4).

A few chapters later, the Israelites are engaged in the building of the portable tabernacle that is to accompany them in their journey through the wilderness. Once again they use gold earrings, this time for positive purposes. This prompted the sages to observe: "With earrings they sinned, and with earrings they were restored to God's favor."

In this pithy comment, the rabbis called attention to the ambivalent character of our wealth. It is morally neutral. Whether it is good or bad depends on the purposes to which we put it.

But is this not true of most things? There are few things that are good or bad in themselves. They derive their powers to curse or to bless from what we make of them.

Consider, for example, the matter of religion itself. The word comes from a root that means "to bind together," and we usually think of religion as a cohesive force helping people to feel closer to one another. Too often in history, however, religion has been a divisive influence, promoting intolerance and hatred and setting people against one another. Too many people have just enough religion to hate those who differ, but not enough to love them.

We all thrill when a new invention is announced, but the road to hell, it has been said, is paved with good inventions.

Science has laid bare for us many of nature's secrets and has enabled man to walk on the moon, but it has also given us the means to blow up the world. In the hands of the Nazis, science was used to build more economical gas chambers.

Our personal qualities also can be pluses or minuses, depending
. . . Frankness can become cruelty; confidence can become arrogance; caution can become timidity.

On the other hand, stubbornness can become perseverance; extravagance can become generosity; and fear of failure can lead to success.

A golden calf or a tabernacle—what shall we fashion with our gifts?

The Perils of Prosperity

Oscar Wilde once made an observation that is worth pondering in a success-oriented society. With characteristic irony, he wrote: "Anybody can sympathize with the sufferings of a friend, but it requires a very fine nature to sympathize with a friend's success."

Wilde alerted us to the truth that in life we face two dangers. The first is that we may not get what we want; the second is that we may. Success, no less than failure, has its own built-in perils.

That the ancient rabbis were also sensitive to the risks inherent in success is reflected in a comment they made on one of the best-known passages of the Bible, the "Priestly Blessing," which begins with the verse: "May the Lord bless you and keep you" (Numbers 6:24).

One of the sages interpreted this verse as follows: "May God bless you"—with earthly possessions—"and keep you"—may He keep these possessions from possessing you. May He shield you against the destructive effects that too often follow prosperity.

What this rabbi was saying in effect is that it requires a strong moral constitution to withstand an attack of prosperity. What are some of the perils of prosperity?

When the sun of bright fortune smiles on us, we are tempted to self-glorification. How clever I am! How astute and resourceful I am! We become "self-made men," and we are all too prone to worship our maker.

Another danger is that we come to worship material possessions, sacrificing health, honor, principles, and family to obtain them. When "things are in the saddle," they ride us; they do not belong to us, we belong to them.

In our preoccupation with material riches, we are also in danger of growing insensitive to the riches of the spirit. These can be cultivated even in the soil of adversity. The anonymous author of the following piece reminds us that if we do not get what we want, perhaps true success means learning to want what we get.

I asked God for strength, that I might achieve; I was made weak, that I might learn humbly to obey. I asked for health, that I might do greater things; I was given infirmity, that I might do better things. I asked for riches, that I might be happy; I was given poverty, that I might be wise. I asked for power, that I might have the praise of men; I was given weakness, that I might feel the need of God. I asked for all things, that I might enjoy life; I was given life, that I might enjoy all things. I got nothing that I asked for—but everything I had hoped for. Almost despite myself, my unspoken prayers were answered. I am among all men, most richly blessed.

What If We Can't Love Our Neighbor?

A newspaper cartoon shows a rather testy-looking woman greeting her minister on the way out of church. The caption reads, "I'd like to see *you* love *my* neighbors!"

She has a point—a point we usually prefer to overlook. We quote the biblical verse "Thou shalt love thy neighbor as thyself" (Leviticus 19:18), we nod our heads approvingly, and then we have that warm, self-righteous feeling as we add, "Yes, I believe in that."

Some people who profess no religious faith at all will frequently explain themselves: "For me, loving your neighbor as yourself is my religion."

If only it were as easy to observe that command as it is to quote it! But as the unconvinced woman reminded the preacher, it isn't all that easy.

Is it really possible for us to relate in love to some of the people we actually know? To *all* of them? Do we love all our relatives?

A deeper question—how much do we really love ourselves? Are we all that lovable? Is it a simple matter for all who know us to love us?

As we stop to reflect on one of the most widely acclaimed Jewish teachings, we realize that it is more easily professed than practiced. As an ideal toward which to aim, it is lofty and pure, but as a guide to daily living, it is far from practical.

There is another serious weakness in this biblical injunction. Can human relations be guided by love alone? Love is an emotion, and we cannot always control our emotions, even with the best of intentions.

If we feel no love for our neighbor, what then?

The answer is provided by the majestic words "Justice, justice shall you pursue" (Deuteronomy 16:20).

We may not be able to control our feelings, but we can and must control our actions. We may not be able to give our neighbor love, but we are never permitted to withhold justice from him. This much we owe him no matter how we feel about him.

And if we avoid harming him in any way, the feeling of love may come later.

John Ruskin, the nineteenth-century English essayist, seemed to be addressing himself to this very theme when he wrote: "If we do justice to our brother even though we may not like him, we will come to love him; but if we do injustice to him because we do not love him, we will come to hate him."

If we do take seriously the thundering biblical command "Justice shall you pursue," we may come at last to love one another. If we do not, then love can wait. Justice cannot.

Promises and Piecrusts

The English satirist Jonathan Swift once made the cynical observation that "promises and piecrusts are made to be broken." Swift had probably seen ample evidence of fractured promises, and so have we.

But however casually we may sometimes treat the plighted word, deep down we do feel, as we have been taught, that a man's word should indeed be his bond, and that a person who cannot be trusted to honor a promise cannot be trusted at all. Our noblest instincts endorse the biblical teaching: "When a man vows a vow . . . he shall not break his word; he shall do according to all that proceeds out of his mouth" (Numbers 30:3).

Judaism took this teaching so seriously that the most sacred day of the Jewish year, the Day of Atonement, is ushered in with a prayer that deals with promises and vows. That prayer, Kol Nidre, dramatically reminds us that promises are not piecrusts.

Among the best-known lines of Robert Frost are: "The woods are lovely, dark and deep. /But I have promises to keep,/ And miles to go before I sleep./ . . ." Frost was once asked what promises he had in mind when he wrote those lines. The poet replied, "Oh, promises to myself and promises to my ancestors."

All of us, like the poet, have promises to keep to ourselves. And I am not thinking only of promises we put into words or write out over our signatures. Some of the most sacred promises are made without words in the silent sanctuary of the soul. There are the promises we have made to ourselves: to surrender a destructive habit, to abandon some shabby and unworthy practice, to effect a reconciliation with a friend or relative, to become more attentive parents and more devoted mates, to give more time to things of the spirit. How many of these promises have we treated like piecrusts?

There are other unspoken promises to ourselves. We are each endowed at birth with all sorts of magnificent potentialities. There is within us a capacity for idealism, a yearning for truth and beauty and nobility, a sensitivity to the needs and dreams of other people.

In the hopeful dawn of youth, we feel these stirrings inside us and we promise to bring them to life. And yet so often, as the years pass by, we permit these promises to be swept under the rug of expediency. We chalk them up to immaturity and we go on to live "more realistically." Then there comes a moment of honest self-confrontation when we take stock of the unkept promises and we are moved to confess, as did F. Scott Fitzgerald when he wrote, "I have been only a mediocre steward of my talent."

We have promises to keep and miles to go before we sleep.

Let's Place Our Bets Carefully

The man sitting on the park bench facing the synagogue was a picture of dejection. His shabby clothes looked as if he had slept in them, and his tired face was covered by a heavy growth. Overcome by pity for the derelict, the rabbi pressed a five-dollar bill into his hand, whispered, "Godspeed," and was gone. Several hours later the stranger burst into the rabbi's study and, with obvious delight, threw a fistful of bills on the rabbi's desk.

"Rabbi," he exclaimed, "Godspeed paid fourteen to one!"

A suggestive truth leaps at us from this humorous anecdote. Like the charitable rabbi, we are all gamblers—whether we realize it or not. Even those of us who have strong moral objections to gambling with money gamble all the time with much more precious stakes.

When we fall in love, we gamble. When we decide to have a child, we gamble. When we choose a career, we gamble. We don't usually think of scientists as gamblers, but in the laboratory the odds against the researcher are often monstrously high and the chips are long, hard sacrificial years—the very stuff of life.

On August 31, 1909, the German-Jewish chemist and bacteriologist Paul Ehrlich discovered his "magic bullet," the most effective cure for syphilis. He called the compound 606 because it had been preceded by 605 failures!

The following year he was honored by his colleagues. When he rose to acknowledge their lavish tributes, Ehrlich said, "You say a great work of the mind, a wonderful scientific achievement! My dear colleagues, for seven years of misfortune I had one moment of good luck."

His biographer writes of him: "At bottom Paul Ehrlich was a gambler, as who of the great line of microbe hunters has not been?" Ehrlich bet on humanity, and his long shot paid off.

If we trace any blessing far enough back, we usually will find that we owe it to someone who gambled for it and won.

We enjoy the blessing of freedom because Moses bet his life on it. Columbus discovered America because he bet his life on the belief that the world was round. More than we usually realize it, we owe so much to those who risked so much. When we decide to live moral and ethical lives, we gamble. We bet on honesty to win over dishonesty; on kindness to prevail over cruelty; on justice to defeat injustice; on peace to conquer war; on brotherhood to triumph over hatred; on faith in God to overcome despair.

We are as big as the things on which we bet our lives. So let's place our bets carefully.

Testing

One of the most dramatic events related in the Bible is the binding of Isaac. The entire stirring narrative can be read in the twenty-second chapter of Genesis. For reflection I would like to zero in on the phrase the Bible uses in introducing the story: "God tested Abraham."

Nachmanides, a medieval Bible commentator, pointed out that the omniscient God needed no tests to determine the dimensions of Abraham's devotion. When the Bible says, "God tested Abraham," it is expressing the situation from the point of view of Abraham. In other words, it was Abraham who looked upon this challenge as a test. He felt that his character was being plumbed, his stature was being measured.

Nor was this the only time that Abraham felt himself being tested. Jewish tradition teaches us that Abraham was tested no fewer than ten times. Again and again when a heavy burden was laid upon him, when a risky assignment was given to him, when a luring temptation was placed before him, Abraham felt himself being tested. Each trial was an opportunity to demonstrate, to himself and to his God, the stuff of which he was made.

Is this perhaps the secret of his radiant life? Is this the attitude we need if our lives are to be the meaningful adventures we know they can be? Must we too learn to regard life as a classroom and every experience as a quiz whose purpose it is to determine not what we know but what we are?

Our sages correctly observed: "There is no creature whom God does not test." We are all tested. We are always tested. Whether we are aware of it or not, life constantly springs little quizzes on us. Every day is examination day. Life is like a candid camera—it doesn't wait for us to pose.

The doctor confronting his patient is having his dedication tested. The lawyer consulting with his client is having his integrity tested. The preacher preparing his sermon is having his honesty tested. The teacher preparing her lesson is having her devotion tested. The businessman on the telephone, the carpenter building a shed, the mechanic under the car, the painter on the scaffold—each is having his character tested.

When a neighbor has been bruised, our kindness is tested. When he has been blessed, our generosity is tested. When we have been hurt, our forgiveness is tested. When we have hurt, our humility is tested. Trouble tests our courage. Temptation tests our strength. Friendship tests our loyalty. Failure tests our perseverance.

To look upon life as a series of tests means to bring to it at every time the finest of which we are capable; to keep ourselves always in top moral condition; to realize the enormous possibilities for good or for ill inherent in each situation, regardless of how unspectacular or humdrum it may appear.

Ralph Waldo Emerson put this truth in striking words: "It is one of the illusions that the present hour is not the critical, decisive hour. Write it on your heart, that every day is the best day of the year. No man has earned anything rightly until he knows that every day is doomsday. Today is a king in disguise. . . . Let us not be deceived, let us unmask the king as he passes."

Who Is Handicapped?

During the hot days of July 1981, nine handicapped adventurers captured the headlines and won our hearts. Five of them were blind, two were deaf, one was an epileptic, and the last had an artificial leg. These intrepid nine conquered snow-capped Mount Rainier, which towers 14,410 feet in forbidding, defiant majesty. When word reached us from Washington State that they had successfully completed their climb to the frozen summit and had safely negotiated the treacherous descent, we all stood taller.

The breathtaking accomplishment of these people was a dramatic demonstration of the power of the human will to triumph over massive obstacles. It was also a much-needed reassurance to all who are handicapped. And when I say, "all who are handicapped," I really mean to include all of us as well, since in one way or another, each of us is handicapped.

On the very day the mountain climbers completed their heart-pumping triumph, a forty-year-old man had come to see me in my study. In appearance, he is tall, handsome, vigorous, well groomed. Except for the disturbed look in his light blue eyes, he might be a matinee idol. All his organs and limbs are intact. But he is an extremely unhappy man.

He has survived a divorce and then the death of his second wife some years later. He is still mourning her terribly. His efforts to enter into new relationships with women have proven disappointing. He is so down on himself that some days it takes all his strength just to get out of bed. His work on the job is perfunctory and far below par. He is in real danger of losing that job. Question: Is this man handicapped?

One of the most moving scenes in the play *Butterflies Are Free* shows a young girl about to desert her blind lover. She justifies her flight by shouting at him, "Because you're blind, you're crippled." To this taunt the young man replies out of his darkness, "No, I'm not crippled. I'm sightless but not crippled. You are crippled because you can't commit yourself to anyone."

Not all handicaps are physical and not all handicaps are visible, but to be human is to be handicapped, to be flawed. "There is a crack," wrote Emerson, "in everything God made.",

Some of us are handicapped by a disturbing sense of inferiority and inadequacy. Some of us carry childhood scars inflicted by constant criticism and bitter rejection.

Some of us feel unworthy of being loved; others cannot give love. Some of us are burdened by guilt; others are filled with rage. Some of us are consumed by envy; others are driven by greed.

Some of us have forfeited our self-respect; others never acquired it. Some of us are battered by fear; others are buffeted by frustration and failure. Some of us are imprisoned by selfishness; others are enslaved by alcohol or pills. Some of us suffer heartaches because of our children; others are tormented by our parents. Some of us carry within us the gray ash of burned-out dreams; others are haunted by fractured hopes and unfulfilled promises. Some of us are convinced of our own worthlessness; others are persuaded of life's meaninglessness.

According to an old Italian story, in Naples there was a man who could not shake off a feeling of deep depression, so he went to a doctor for help. After a thorough examination, the physician said to the patient, "There is really nothing physically wrong with you. May I suggest that you go to the theater tonight to see the great comedian Carlini. He brings laughter to large crowds at every performance. He will surely drive away your sadness."

At these words, the patient burst into tears. "But, Doctor," he sobbed, "I am Carlini!"

To know that being handicapped is the common lot of each and every one of us may make our own handicaps a little easier to accept. We have not been singled out by a malicious fate for special abuse. We are simply paying the price of being human.

And before we become too envious of the other fellow who seems to have it all, we might pause to reflect that he too carries his own shabby secrets and dark sorrows, his own heavy, invisible handicaps.

Of course, we must take care to ensure that we do not use our handicaps as an alibi to justify failure. All human progress and achievements were accomplished not in the absence of handicaps but in the face of them. "I thank God for my handicaps," wrote Helen Keller, "for through them I have found myself, my work, my God."

One of the blind mountain climbers explained the success of the adventure quite simply: "We had a lot of help from each other on the trip." Our own perilous journey through life is an adventure filled with obstacles, risks, and pitfalls that each of us must negotiate burdened as we are by an assortment of handicaps. We can, however, succeed. But we need a lot of help from one another on the trip.

Say Yes to Life

Stories of two paraplegics were in the news about one week apart. One was Kenneth B. Wright, a high-school football star and, later, an avid wrestler, boxer, hunter, and skin diver. A broken neck sustained in a wrestling match in 1979 left him paralyzed from the chest down. He underwent therapy, and his doctors were hopeful that one day he would be able to walk with the help of braces and crutches.

But, apparently, the former athlete could not reconcile himself to his physical disability. He prevailed upon two of his best friends to take him in his wheelchair to a wooded area, where they left him alone with a twelve-gauge shotgun. After they left, he held the shotgun to his abdomen and pulled the trigger. Kenneth Wright, twenty-four, committed suicide.

The second paraplegic in the news was Jim McGowan. Thirty years ago, at the age of nineteen, Jim was stabbed and left paralyzed from the middle of his chest down. He is now confined to a wheelchair. But he came to our attention recently when he made a successful parachute jump, landing on target in the middle of Lake Wallenpaupack in the Pocono Mountains of Pennsylvania.

Soon afterward, I spoke with Jim and learned a number of other things about him. He lives alone, cooks his own meals, washes his own clothes, and cleans his own house. He drives himself wherever he goes in his specially equipped automobile. He has written three books, and he took the photographs for the first book published on the history of wheelchair sports.

When I asked Jim how he managed to do so much with so little, he answered, "It wasn't easy. I had my years of darkness, and it took a long time to get there. Then I came to the conclusion that I am ultimately responsible for my life. Since I am responsible for my life, I'm going to make it as beautiful as I can."

No shotgun, please.

No one has the right to sit in judgment of the disabled athlete who threw in the towel. Who knows what any one of us would have done in his terrible situation? Long ago, a Jewish sage warned us: "Do not judge your fellow man until you are in his place."

But Jim McGowan's heroic response to the same disability is surely a much-needed reminder of the resilience of the human spirit, of our God-given ability to cope with—and to triumph over—difficult or even impossible-seeming circumstances. One of the heavy burdens of being human is the need to make choices—choices that are often as desperately difficult as they are decisive. Edwin Markham, the twentieth-century American poet, wrote of these agonizing dilemmas:

> *I will leave man to make the fateful guess*
> *Will leave him torn between No and Yes*
> *Leave him in the tragic loneliness to choose*
> *With all in life to win or lose.*

The most fateful choices are made in tragic loneliness. In the valley of decision, we stand alone, accompanied only by our haunting fears or our stubborn hopes, by dread despair or gritty faith.

Yet, though we appear to stand solitary, in truth we are accompanied by the tall and brave spirits who have stood where we stand and who, when torn between "No" and "Yes" have said "Yes" to life and its infinite possibilities; by those who have had the wisdom to focus not on what they had lost but on what they had left; by those who understood that fate is what life gives to us and that destiny is what we do with what's given; and by those who, therefore, grasped the liberating truth that while we have no control over our fate, we do have an astonishing amount of control over our destiny.

When a blind man was asked by a sympathetic woman, "Doesn't being blind rather color your life?" he answered: "Yes, but, thank God, I can choose the color."

The plane that carried paraplegic Jim McGowan to his historic skydive should also have carried aloft the spirits of the discouraged and the despondent, the defeated and the despairing. If he could soar so high, then who has the right to feel low? To all who find themselves in a time of darkness, Jim's words shine with a luminous radiance: "Since I am responsible for my life, I'm going to make it as beautiful as I can."

This Is the Day

One of my favorite biblical verses, a verse that becomes dearer to me as I grow older, proclaims a truth of which we should be reminded as we greet each new day: "This is the day that the Lord has made; on it let us rejoice and be glad" (Psalms 118:24).

The recognition that each day is another gift from God, that each day is an occasion for joy and gladness, can go a long way toward making us aware of the extraordinary privilege of being alive right here and right now. This awareness can in turn inspire us to live each day more intensely, more fully.

Too much of our living is done in the past or in the future while we neglect the present. But yesterday is a canceled check and tomorrow is a promissory note. Only today is cash at hand for us to spend. "This is the day . . ."

Margaret Storm Jameson, the British novelist, has spoken directly to this theme:

> I believe that only one person in a thousand knows the trick of really living in the present. Most of us spend fifty-nine minutes an hour living in the past, with regret for lost joys, or shame for things badly done (both utterly useless and weakening)—or in a future that we either long for or dread. Yet the past is gone beyond prayer, and every minute we spend in the vain effort to anticipate the future is a moment lost. There is only one world, the world pressing against you at this minute. There is only one minute in which you are alive, this minute—here and now. The only way to live is by accepting each minute as an unrepeatable miracle. Which is exactly what it is—a miracle and unrepeatable.

When our daughters were young and we would start out on a trip, one of them was in the habit of asking about five minutes after we left, "Daddy, are we almost there?" A few minutes later she would ask, "When are we going to get there?" This is a question that is typical of too many of us. When are we going to get there? We are so anxious to get there that we don't enjoy the journey. And we forget that life is a journey and not a destination.

We are always looking ahead to something in the future. We are preparing for graduation, for a profession; we are working to pay off the mortgage; we are looking forward to the children's being independent; we're saving for that new home or the new car. And we wonder when we are going to get there. And then one day it suddenly dawns upon us that we've been there all along and that we should have enjoyed the journey a lot more. We should have paid more attention to some of the lovely scenes that we were passing en route. We should have lived more in each today.

One of the people whom I have known for many years retired from his business not long ago. I remember how eagerly he looked forward to retirement and how zealously he applied himself to making his retirement possible and comfortable. An extraordinary amount of sacrifice and self-denial went into the planning for this retirement. But when I spoke with him recently I had the depressing feeling that retirement turned out to be a lot less fun than he had imagined it would be. And I could not help wondering, too, how many todays he missed for this tomorrow, which was finally today.

This is part and parcel of the problem of constantly asking, "When are we going to get there?" When we get there, we may find that there is no "there" there and all the while we were missing the fun of the journey. We were always going to live tomorrow, and in the meanwhile all those precious, irretrievable todays slipped away.

Life is a journey, not a destination, and happiness is not "there" but here; not tomorrow, but today. Let's not live by the edict of the White Queen in *Alice in Wonderland*: "Jam yesterday and jam tomorrow but never jam today." Today is not a parenthesis between yesterday and tomorrow. Good things can happen, do happen, and should happen today, if we make sure that they happen; if we learn how to live today.

"This is the day the Lord has made; on it let us rejoice and be glad."

We Wait Too Long

Watch the faces of people who celebrate a birthday, an anniversary, a new year, and see if you do not detect a certain wistfulness in their expressions, a measure of tentativeness in their joy. They seem to follow the biblical advice to "rejoice with trembling."

Life's arithmetic is not simple. Every addition is also a subtraction. When we add a year to those we have already lived, we subtract a year from those remaining to be lived. So the privilege of reaching another milestone is accompanied by the sobering reminder of life's relentless flight.

There is therefore an added sense of urgency to the advice Teddy Kollek, Jerusalem's dynamic mayor, gives in his autobiography, *For Jerusalem*. He recommends an Eleventh Commandment: "Thou shalt not be patient."

At first blush this bit of advice flies in the face of one of the most universally admired virtues—patience. "He that can have patience," wrote Benjamin Franklin, "can have what he wills."

And yet as we reflect on Kollek's words, they seem to contain a pungent wisdom that can serve as a much-needed antidote to our too-human tendency to procrastinate. The truth about us is that in too many vital areas of life we wait too long.

We often wait too long to do what must be done today, in a world that gives us only one day at a time, without any assurance of tomorrow. While lamenting that our days are few, we act as though we had an endless supply of time.

We wait too long to discipline ourselves and to take charge of our lives. We feed ourselves the vain delusion that it will be easier to uproot tomorrow the debasing habits we permit to tyrannize us today and that grow more deeply entrenched each day they remain in power.

We wait too long to show kindness. F. Scott Fitzgerald, the laureate of "the lost generation" created by World War I, wrote to a friend in a time of sadness, "Pray, do write to me. A few lines soon are better than a three-decker novel a month hence."

We wait too long to speak the words of forgiveness that should be spoken, to set aside the hatreds that should be banished, to express thanks, to give encouragement, to offer comfort.

We wait too long to be charitable. Too much of our giving is delayed until much of the need has passed and the joy of giving has largely been diminished.

A magazine cartoon shows two old women draped in rags shivering over a meager fire. One asks, "What are you thinking about?" The other answers, "About the nice warm clothes the rich will be giving us next summer."

We wait too long to be parents to our children—forgetting how brief is the time during which they are children, how swiftly life urges them on and away. We wait too long to express our concern for parents, siblings, and dear ones. Who knows how soon it will be too late?

We wait too long to read the books, to listen to the music, and to see the art waiting to enlarge our minds, to enrich our spirits, and to expand our souls.

We wait too long to utter the prayers that are waiting to cross our lips, to perform the duties waiting to be discharged, to show the love that may no longer be needed tomorrow. We wait too long in the wings when life has a part for us to play on the stage.

God, too, is waiting—waiting for us to stop waiting, and to begin to do now all the things for which this day and this life have been given to us.

Failure—the Line of Least Persistence

One of Adlai Stevenson's favorite stories concerned a man who was being interviewed on his hundredth birthday. Naturally, he was asked to what he attributed his longevity.

He answered, "I have never smoked, imbibed alcohol, nor over-eaten. I go to bed early and I get up early."

"You know," said the reporter, "I had an uncle who lived exactly that way and he only lived to the age of ninety. To what do you attribute that?"

The old man replied, "He just didn't keep it up long enough."

In the old man's humorous response, we find a sad reflection on one of our most common human failings—a lack of perseverance and persistence. We set out for great goals with matching enthusiasm, but we just don't keep it up long enough. And when we lose the will and the determination to persevere in our quest, we have lost perhaps the single most important requirement for success. Failure is the line of least persistence.

"Nothing in the world," wrote Calvin Coolidge, "can take the place of persistence. Talent will not; nothing is more common than unsuccessful men with talent. Genius will not; unrewarded genius is almost a proverb. Education will not; the world is full of educated derelicts. Persistence and determination alone are omnipotent."

Persistence is crucial not only for reaching outward goals but also for retaining our inner visions.

One of the glorious characteristics of youth is its capacity for bold dreams, its ability to believe in the good and the true and the beautiful. But as we grow older we tend to become weary and cynical, and we shed the high resolves and noble dreams that set us aflame in our tender years.

Reflecting on this change, Dr. Albert Schweitzer wrote:

We believed once in the victory of truth; but we do not now. We believed in goodness; we do not now. We were zealous for justice, but we are not so now. We trusted in the power of

92

kindness, peaceableness; we do not now. We were capable of enthusiasm, but we are not so now. To get through the shoals and storms of life more easily we have lightened our craft, throwing overboard what we thought could be spared. But it was really our stock of food and drink of which we deprived ourselves; our craft is now easier to manage but we ourselves are in a decline.

It would be most instructive for all of us, and very humbling for many of us, if we compared our goals today with the ideals we cherished ten or twenty years ago. How many lives have suffered a progressive deterioration of motive, a gradual contraction of purpose and shrinking of the horizons?

How many of us went forth in our chosen vocations dedicated to justice, and then decided to play it safe?

How many of us swore in our youthful hearts that we would try to heal the hurt of humanity, only to find ourselves preoccupied exclusively with our own comforts and luxuries?

How many of us stood on the threshold of parenthood and vowed that we would execute faithfully the sacred responsibility it confers, only to become absentee parents who give our children everything except what they need most—ourselves?

How many of us promised ourselves that when we had more time, when life's economic demands would become less insistent, we would take seriously our religious obligations? Then, we came upon more leisure than we had ever had, we became more comfortable than we had ever been, and we decided to invest our added time and resources exclusively in amusement, recreation, and self-delight.

Dr. Schweitzer, who sensitively diagnosed our malady, also prescribed a cure. He advised us, "The great secret of success is to go through life as a man who never gets used up. Grow into your ideals so that life can never rob you of them."

Remember, a diamond is just a piece of coal that stayed on the job.

One Day at a Time

We took a coffee break on the turnpike and decided that things would go faster at the counter. The nameplate on her uniform read "Tex," and her smile was warm and friendly. The patrons were few, and she had lots of time to pour out her heart, together with the two cups of coffee.

She hadn't always been a waitress. She was a housewife raising two young boys when her husband was killed in an accident. Suddenly her whole world caved in. In addition to her own sense of loss and desolation, there was the awesome responsibility of being father and mother to her sons.

She was gripped by panic and a paralyzing sense of helplessness. How would she manage all those stark, frightening years that stretched bleakly ahead of her? How would she care for herself and the two boys?

For the longest time she sat at home brooding and worrying. "Then one night," she said, "as I tossed sleeplessly, it came to me. I realized that I didn't have to solve all my problems all at once. All I had to do was to get through one day at a time. And for one day I could be strong enough, smart enough, and tough enough. That thought helped me to see it through."

What happened to the boys? Today one is a physician, the other is in medical school; and Mama serves the counter trade.

Tex poured out a lot of wisdom with her coffee. I've had occasion to pass along her advice in all kinds of difficult circumstances, and I have even kept some for personal use.

In times of trouble and tragedy, we deepen our anxiety and our pain if we try to look too far ahead. The climb seems so steep, the road is strewn with so many hurdles, we simply don't see how we're going to make it. But if we can look just one day ahead and try to muster sufficient courage and faith for that one day, we usually find that our inner resources are equal to the demand.

"The hero," wrote Emerson, "is no braver than an ordinary man, but he is brave five minutes longer." In this sense we can all strive for heroism—to be brave not for a lifetime, not for years or even for months—but just for five minutes longer.

It is worth noting that in the beloved twenty-third psalm the Bible says: "Yea though I *walk* through the valley of the shadow of death." We can neither fly over the valley, detour around it, nor run through it. We have to walk. One heavy step at a time. One lonely night at a time, one empty day at a time. Then somehow, in God's goodness, the days become weeks, the weeks add up to months, and the months turn into years.

But we cannot live years at a time. As Tex said—one day at a time. And if we do indeed persevere, patiently but resolutely, breaking time into manageable little pieces, we often discover the surprising truth captured by the anonymous poet:

> *These things are beautiful beyond belief:*
> *The pleasant weakness that comes after pain,*
> *The radiant greenness that comes after rain,*
> *The deepened faith that follows after grief,*
> *And the awakening to love again.*

Nothing There

Great discoveries are usually made by people who are so passionately committed to their quest that they can withstand the discouragement of those who are convinced that the goals they seek are only illusions. The discovery of our own country is a striking case in point. Christopher Columbus bravely ventured forth on his intrepid voyage because he was strong enough to resist the defeatist counsel of those who had themselves tried unsuccessfully to do what he set out to do.

Even before Columbus, there was a theory that if you sailed far enough westward across the ocean you would reach land. Well, a group of Portuguese sailors ventured out on the Atlantic, traveled about fifty or a hundred miles, and then returned and pronounced their considered judgment: "There's nothing there." Mind you, there was out there a whole new world to find for those who had the courage and the perseverance to sail on, and here they were after one abortive effort rendering the verdict: Nothing there!

The mistake of the Portuguese sailors did not die with them. In so many vital areas of life we, too, make abbreviated voyages of discovery, turn back, and pronounce: Nothing there!

Consider, for example, how many Americans resemble the Portuguese sailors where marriage is concerned. We've heard a theory that if we set sail on the sea of matrimony we will discover the continent of fulfillment and happiness. And so we launch our boats, venture forth briefly, run into a few squalls or choppy seas, and head back for shore muttering dejectedly: Nothing there!

We live in an age that teaches us to expect that we'll get what we want when we want it. As a result, we are altogether unprepared when we find that marriage requires flexibility, adjustment, experimentation, faith—and patience. Yet it's only when the seas are choppy and the winds grow turbulent that the mastery of the helmsman is truly tested. It is easy and tempting to head for the shore and cry: Nothing there! But the prize lies in the other direction.

There is another important area in which we resemble the Portuguese sailors. More of us than are aware of it are guilty of underestimating ourselves. We may never actually think such thoughts or voice them, but we often pass that kind of scathing judgement on ourselves. Nothing there! We avoid taking on new duties for fear that we will be unable to discharge them adequately. We run away from challenges because we have little confidence in our ability to meet them squarely. So often in the aftermath of a great emergency we're surprised to have found ourselves equal to the heavy demands laid upon us, and we say, perhaps with wonder, "I didn't know I had that in me."

Let us but persevere in our voyages of self-discovery and we will be delighted to discover more courage, more strength, more resilience of spirit than we ever suspected we possessed. There is indeed something there.

And where our religion is concerned, far too many of us have passed the hasty verdict: Nothing there! I have heard otherwise intelligent and judicious people deliver themselves of conclusions that have no visible means of support. Thus a man turns his back on his ancestral faith because: "I went to a service once and it left me cold." Another abandons the precious legacy of centuries because "religion is superstition." Shades of the Portuguese sailors.

Sail on, dear friends, on the sea of knowledge. Probe, study, and find out why so many people have found their faiths, as we Jews have ever found ours, to be "a tree of life to those who grasp hold of it." There is indeed something great and powerful there!

When You Come to the End of Your Rope

The devil once decided that he would retire from business and sell all his diabolical devices. On the day of the sale, all his tools were put on display, each with a price tag.

One rather plain-looking and much-worn tool was priced considerably higher than the others. The devil was asked what it was.

"That's Discouragement," he said.

"Why is it priced so high?"

"Because," the devil answered, "it is more useful to me than all the others. I use it to get into a man's mind, and once inside I can use him to do my work. It is greatly worn because it is my favorite tool. I have used it on nearly everybody, yet few people know that it belongs to me."

Well, according to the fable, the devil's price for Discouragement was so high that nobody bought it. And he's still using it.

I thought of this parable as I reread the biblical portion that tells how the Israelites in the wilderness reacted when they heard the report of ten of the twelve men who had surveyed the land of Canaan.

The ten had said that the inhabitants of Canaan were veritable giants. Compared to them, the Israelites were like grasshoppers. "We are not able to go up against the people for they are stronger than we" (Numbers 13:31).

Joshua and Caleb tried to persuade the people that they could indeed conquer the land. Their efforts were in vain. Totally discouraged by the majority report, the Israelites wept and wailed, and they were doomed to perish in the desert.

The situation was not hopeless, only the people were. Fear had defeated them. Without hope for their future, they had no power in the present. When they lost hope, they lost heart. They could not achieve because they did not believe.

Who can calculate how much of human failure is due not to efforts that went wrong but to efforts that were withheld? Heaven only knows how many opportunities were lost because timid, frightened, and discouraged people did not have the strength to try.

I once listened to a long tale of woe from a young man who had gotten into much more trouble than he felt he could handle. He saw no way out. He made a gesture of despair as he sighed, "I'm at the end of the rope."

At that moment, I recalled the advice a member of my congregation had heard from her father: "When you come to the end of the rope, make a knot and hold on."

Let's not give the devil easy victories.

Shortcuts to Distant Goals

A modern American was overheard offering a crisp prayer: "Dear God, please grant me patience. And I want it right now."

He was a faithful reflection of our assembly-line, speed-addicted "now" generation. We want what we want when we want it. We want it yesterday, today at the very latest; certainly not tomorrow. *Instant* is a key word in our vocabulary.

The frenetic pace of contemporary life shows through some of the verbs we use to describe our daily actions. We leap out of bed, we gulp our coffee, we bolt our food, we whiz into town, we dash to the office, we tear for home, and we drop dead. We travel at twice the speed of sound and half the speed of sense.

There is, for us, an especially crucial message in the biblical passage that tells of the way the Israelites traveled when they went out of Egypt. "God did not lead them by way of the land of the Philistines, although it was nearer; for God said, 'The people may have a change of heart when they see war, and return to Egypt.' So God led the people roundabout by way of the wilderness at the Sea of Reeds" (Exodus 13:17–18).

Notice what the Bible is telling us. God deliberately avoided leading the Israelites on the shorter road. He took them on the long road because in His divine wisdom He knew that the short road to freedom could also become the quick road back to slavery. And so He led them "roundabout." Thus they—and we—were given the inescapable message: Beware of shortcuts to distant goals.

Happiness in marriage is a distant goal. There was a time when young people were warned that if they married in haste they would repent at leisure. This is no longer true. More and more young people are repenting in haste. They are too impatient to make the adjustments that marriage inevitably entails. They cannot wait to learn the tolerance that marriage always demands. They don't have the time to achieve the understanding that never comes quickly. They have not been taught that while love may

100

come suddenly, happiness is a distant goal to which there is no shortcut.

The development of character is a distant goal. Goethe, the nineteenth-century German poet, once revealed the truth in this matter when he said, "Life is a quarry out of which we are to mold and chisel and complete a character." Notice all those time-consuming verbs. Character is distilled out of our daily confrontation with temptation, out of our regular response to the call of duty. It is formed as we learn to cherish principles and to submit to self-discipline. Character is the sum total of all the little decisions, the small deeds, the daily reactions to the choices that confront us. Character is not obtained instantly. We have to mold and hammer and forge ourselves into character. It is a distant goal to which there is no shortcut.

A genuine faith in God is a distant goal. We do not believe in instant conversions or spontaneous spiritual combustion. Like Jonah's gourd, that which grows in a day perishes in a day. A genuine faith in God, an appreciation of the wealth of our heritage and its noble beauty, have to be acquired slowly, painstakingly, in regular daily doses.

Religion is a quiet dimension of daily living; it is not a spectacular explosion. Its symbol is the soft eternal light, not the dramatic firecracker.

The Danger of Staying the Same Size

One of the central prayers offered in the synagogue on the High Holy Days expresses the hope that God's sovereignty will be established over all the earth, and then "every creature will know that You created it; every living thing will recognize that You fashioned it."

Why is it important that we should each look upon ourselves as God's creatures? What difference does it really make?

Abraham J. Heschel, one of this century's most celebrated interpreters of Judaism, once pointed out that in the Jewish view, man is man not because of what he has in common with the earth but because of what he has in common with God. The Greek thinkers sought to understand man as part of the universe; the prophets sought to understand man as a partner of God. To consider ourselves as God's partners is a challenge to continue to create with God that creature God meant us to be.

In one of Wallace Stegner's novels, *Second Growth,* there is a scene dealing with our theme. It takes place in a small town in Vermont where opportunities for young people are limited. A teacher becomes interested in a young boy who shows a great deal of promise. She encourages him to leave the little town and to look elsewhere for greater educational opportunities.

"I'd take this chance to go to college if I were you," she tells him. "There won't be much else we could teach you around here. You would stay the same size all your life."

The risk of staying the same size all our lives is as great in a madly bustling metropolis as it is in a sleepy little town. And it is not only our minds that must continue to grow. To reach our full God-given potential, we must mature emotionally and spiritually as well.

Americans today spend billions on diet foods, diet drinks, exercise, and recreational activities. All these testify to our justifiable fear of growing in the wrong places and in the wrong ways as we grow older.

What we need is the greater fear that in some vital ways we stop growing altogether. Where our truly human dimensions are concerned—the dimensions of the mind, heart, and soul—we must not stay the same size all our lives.

In Hamlet, Shakespeare says, "We know what we are, but we know not what we may be." Perhaps I would put it a little differently. When we truly know who we are, God's creatures, who will dare to set a limit on what we may be?

The Principal Character Is Waiting to Appear

It is told of Thomas Edison that he once stood looking at the ocean and wept as he gazed upon the waves because there was so much throbbing energy going to waste.

A waste far more worthy of our tears is the enormous energy within us that never gets channeled, the love that is never expressed, the kindness that never surfaces, the compassion and tenderness that are never awakened.

Dr. Abraham Maslow, the noted psychologist, has estimated that the average human being achieves only 7 percent of his potential.

Would anyone be content with such a slim percentage of success in any field of endeavor? I don't imagine any farmer would be too happy nor would he win any ribbons at the county fair if his wheat fields or his apple orchards yielded only 7 percent of their potential. Should we rest content with such a meager human harvest?

Among his literary remains, Nathaniel Hawthorne left some notebooks that contain random ideas he jotted down as they occurred to him. One of the short entries reads as follows: "Suggestion for a story—story in which the principal character simply never appears."

Unhappily, this is the story of too many lives. The principal character simply never appears. The person we might grow into, the human being we might become, doesn't show up.

Our potential greatness lies unrealized, the splendor remains imprisoned, the promise unfulfilled. Our lives develop a static character.

We stop growing morally, spiritually, and intellectually. We do not expand our sympathies. We do not enlarge our interests. We do not further our knowledge. We do not strengthen our self-control. We remain essentially where we were last year, five years ago, twenty years ago.

But when our growth is stunted, we find a sense of discontent gnawing at us. We become "sick with unused self," to use the phrase of one observer of the human condition. We remain haunted by the "principal character" who invades our dreams in the night and mars our serenity by day.

In our heart of hearts we each know that we were meant to keep growing as long as we keep breathing. If a seed in its dark restless journey under ground is not content until it breaks through the mountain of soil and strains ever higher toward the sunlight, shall we human beings be content to remain "in the original state of nature"?

Whatever our age, it is a time for us to grow—to become more capable of forgiveness, more sensitive to another's pain, more receptive to criticism, more open to a new idea. We must never forget that the principal character is waiting to appear.

Give Us Bread but Give Us Roses Too

One of the pieces of common folk wisdom that many quote without even suspecting its biblical origin is the oft-heard reminder that "man does not live by bread alone" (Deuteronomy 8:3).

Bread is, of course, basic—truly the proverbial staff of life—and no person who professes a sense of justice has the right to sit down to a meal today without the haunting awareness that hundreds of millions of people are always hungry. In fact, there are more hungry people in the world today than there were people one hundred years ago. Until we can resolve the cruelly ironic situation where hunger exists in the face of abundance, we perpetuate one of the gravest sins against God's creatures.

But after we have said all this, the biblical assertion that we do not live by bread alone reminds us that we human beings have other hungers, too—hungers that do not originate in our physical appetites. The poet J. Oppenheim was one who cried out from such hunger pains. He wrote:

> *Hearts starve as well as bodies:*
> *Give us bread, but give us roses!*

What both the Bible and the poet are saying is that God has built into each of us powerful hungers that simply will not be satisfied by bread alone. We have a deep and abiding hunger for love and affection. Without them we shrivel and die. This is not a poetic exaggeration; it is a truth. We have a great hunger to be needed, to know that we are filling a vital role in some life other than our own, that we are performing a task that enriches the community, that we are making some contribution, however humble, to the sum total of things.

We have a genuine hunger for dignity, for self-respect, for the refreshing sights of goodness and courage and kindness—these to enable us to renew our faith in ourselves and in one another.

We hunger most powerfully to believe that life—yours and mine—is not just "a tale told by an idiot, full of sound and fury, signifying nothing"; but that it does have some vast, enduring, and imperishable meaning.

It is important to be aware of these hungers so that we might better understand the kind of creatures we are and what it takes to make us fully human. We are each endowed with a heart that yearns for nourishment; with a spirit restless in its craving; with a soul forever reaching out for something grander than it has ever known; with a mind demanding food to grow on, to expand, to become enlarged.

To be aware of these hungers is to see ourselves in all the richness and splendor to which authors of the Bible alluded when they wrote that "man does not live by bread alone."

Forgive Us Our Virtues

Nearly five decades ago, Vardis Fisher wrote a novel with the ironic title *Forgive Us Our Virtues*. It is a title calculated to puncture the balloon of moral smugness. It reminds us of the harm we so often inflict with the best of intentions and with the noblest of instincts.

A poignant illustration of this truth is found in the biblical chapters that deal with the bitter feelings that tore apart Jacob's family—a family riddled by gossip, envy, and hatred. Only narrowly do Joseph's brothers avoid killing him; instead, they sell him into slavery. Then they practice the cruelest of all deceptions; they convince Jacob that Joseph is dead.

What was it that so terribly splintered this family? Love! Yes, a father's discriminating love. Jacob, the Bible tells us, "loved Joseph more than all his children . . . and he made him a coat of many colors. And when his brothers saw that their father loved him more than all his brothers, they hated him, and could not speak peaceably to him" (Genesis 37:3-4).

Had Jacob realized the destructive power of his misplaced love, perhaps he might have prayed: "Forgive us our virtues."

One of the distressing truths about human nature is that there is no virtue that cannot be turned into a vice, no quality that is immune to corruption.

Jacob wasn't the last father to distort the virtue of parental love. When I see fathers and mothers express this love by trying to solve all their children's problems, permitting them to carry no burdens, take no risks, make no decisions, shoulder no responsibility, submit to no discipline, I am moved to pray, "Forgive us our virtues."

Surely tolerance is a virtue. But when we become tolerant of the intolerable, when we accept passively circumstances and conditions that should fill us with flaming protest, when we remain calmly indifferent to public corruption and betrayal, surely it is time to pray, "Forgive us our virtues."

There are many such examples. Religious zeal has a nasty way of degenerating into fanaticism. Courage often proves self-destructive by becoming recklessness. Loyalty frequently betrays itself by freezing into blind obedience. Curiosity makes a good scientist but a bad neighbor.

Small wonder then that one observer of human nature has written, "The enterprise of living means reckoning with the ravages of virtue as well as those of vice. The evil in the world comes not only from unbridled wrong but also from unbridled good."

Clergymen never weary of calling attention to our sins. Perhaps it might be helpful to reflect on the words of novelist Peter De Vries: "We know God will forgive us our sins; the question is, what will He think of our virtues?"

The Greatest Treason

The doctor examined the three-pack-a-day smoker and was distressed by the findings. "Look here," the doctor said, "you say you've been a heavy smoker for forty-two years. You see that building across the street? If you had saved all that money you spent on cigarettes, you might own that building today."

"Do you smoke, doctor?" the patient asked.

"No, never did."

"Do you own that building?"

"No!"

"Well, I do."

The doctor was correct in urging his patient to surrender a destructive habit, but instead of speaking to him about preserving his health and his life, he spoke about saving dollar bills. He spoke not with the medical authority of a physician, but with the prudence of a banker. He gave him good advice with a bad reason.

There are two lines by T. S. Eliot that the doctor would have done well to ponder:

> *The last temptation is the greatest treason,*
> *To do the right deed for the wrong reason.*

Eliot's lines are addressed not only to the doctor. Many of us could profitably reflect on them.

How many of us pray for the wrong reasons! We have a "slot machine" approach to prayer. All we have to do is insert a prayer and out will come instant fulfillment, immediate gratification, regardless of whether what we are asking for is moral, ethical, or possible; regardless of whether or not it clashes with the needs and hopes of others.

When what we ask for is denied us, we often abandon prayer as an exercise in futility. We forget that prayer at its highest involves praise and thanksgiving and that its primary concern is not getting but becoming. Our prayers are answered when they enable us to grow toward the person we are capable of being, and live as God would have us live.

How many of us perform our small acts of charity and goodness for the wrong reasons. We expect a kind deed to be rewarded by a kind fate, to preserve us from trouble and misfortune. More than once have I heard this melancholy verdict: "When my mother died, I stopped believing in God. She was such a good person, how could God let this happen to her?"

Goodness does not confer immunity to disease, disaster, or death. It does not guarantee a life without trouble or tragedy. These are the common lot of all of us.

Is there then no reward for living a life of rectitude and uprightness? There is, indeed. We are rewarded not *for* our good deeds but *by* our good deeds. The reward for doing good is becoming a better human being. The greatest compensation for any good deed is simply to have done it. It is inherent in the act itself. Moses Maimonides, the twelfth-century Jewish philosopher, gave us the right reason for doing the right deed: "It is not enough to serve God in the hope of future reward. A man must do right and avoid wrong because he is a man and owes it to his manhood to seek perfection."

His words help us to avoid "the greatest treason." They encourage us to do the right deed for the right reason.

The Very Fine Art of Forgetting

An eight-year-old nephew visited us during his summer vacation. At the evening meal, I invited him to lead us in the Hebrew blessing over the bread. He protested that he had forgotten it. "Forgot it?" I exclaimed in mock surprise. "Why, you just learned it in Hebrew school."

"Uncle Sidney," he explained with a twinkle, "I have a very good forgettery."

Young Ritchie stumbled on an important truth. The power to forget sometimes can be "very good." We often apologize for forgetting things. In Moses' farewell address to his people, he rebukes them for having forgotten something very crucial that they should have remembered: "You forgot the God who brought you forth" (Deuteronomy 32:18).

But important as is the power to remember, no less important is the power to forget. Life as we know it would be unbearable if we were not blessed with a "good forgettery." If we had to live each day burdened with the weight of past griefs and bereavements, if we could not banish from our minds our accumulated failures, fears, and frustrations, if the wounds we suffer on life's battlefield were always raw and gaping—then life would be a curse.

A Jewish legend tells us that when the Almighty finished creating the world and was about to release it, He suddenly realized that He had forgotten an indispensable ingredient without which life could not endure. God had forgotten to include the power to forget. So He called back the world and blessed it with that gift, and then He was satisfied that it was ready for human habitation.

How shall we use the great gift of forgettery? I think we should try to forget those things that, if remembered, would bring out our least attractive traits. We should try to remember those things that, if forgotten, would suppress our nobler instincts. We have suffered wrongs and, also, have inflicted them. Too often we recall the instances when we were the victims; we forget those wherein we were the offenders. Were it not wiser to consign to oblivion the wrong suffered, and to repair, where time yet permits, the wrong inflicted?

All too often we remember with bitterness the unfulfilled promises made to us, but we calmly forget the pledge we made and did not honor, the word we gave and did not keep. Were it not better that we forget the first and remember the second?

The poet put it well indeed:

> *This world would be for us a happier place*
> *And there would be less of regretting,*
> *If we would remember to practice with grace,*
> *The very fine art of forgetting.*

The High Cost of Loving

When I was young, there was a popular song that soothingly assured us that "the best things in life are free." I have since experienced enough to learn that some of the best things in life are prohibitively expensive. Often they appear to be freely given but carry an invisible price tag. Love is one of those things.

Those of us who have lost loved ones have learned in our sorrow that we pay an enormous price for love when it ceases to flow. We pay in the coin of grief, longing, yearning, missing. It hurts so much, doesn't it?

The bitter truth is that every love story has an unhappy ending, and the greater the love the greater the unhappiness when it ends.

Whenever we love someone, we give a hostage to fortune. Whenever we permit someone to become very dear to us, we become vulnerable to disappointment and heartbreak.

What, then, is our choice? Never permit ourselves to love anyone? Never permit anyone to matter to us? To deny ourselves the greatest of all God-given joys?

If loving is expensive, being unloved and unloving costs even more. I believe that even in our grief we can still agree with the sentiment of a contemporary writer: "To love and be loved is to feel the sun from both sides."

And one more consideration can be mentioned. If some fairy angel came to us in our deepest sorrow and offered to remove all our pain and all our longing, but with them would also remove all our memories of the years and the adventures we shared, would we agree to the bargain? Or would we consider those memories so precious, so infinitely dear, that we would hug them close to our hearts and refuse to purchase instant relief by surrendering them?

An ancient Greek legend gives a clue to the choice we would probably make. It tells of a woman who came down to the River Styx where Charon, the gentle ferryman, stood ready to take her to the region of the departed spirits. Charon reminded her that it was her privilege to drink of the waters of Lethe, and that if she did so she would completely forget all that she was leaving behind.

Eagerly she said, "I will forget how I have suffered." To which Charon responded, "But remember, you will also forget how you have rejoiced." Then the woman said, "I will forget my failures." The old ferryman added, "And also your victories." Again the woman said, "I will forget how I have been hurt." "You will also forget," countered Charon, "how you have been loved."

The woman then paused to think the whole matter over, and the story concludes by telling us that she did not drink the waters of Lethe, preferring to hold on to the memory even of her suffering and her sorrow rather than surrender the remembrance of life's joys and loves.

An old Yiddish proverb consoles us in our suffering by reminding us: "Not to have had pain is not to have been human." The pain passes, the memories remain; loved ones leave us, but having had loved ones endures. And we are so much richer and so much enlarged for having paid the high cost of loving.

Four Rs of Repentance

The most solemn time of the year on the Jewish calendar is the High Holy Day season which comes in the early fall. It begins with Rosh Hashanah, the Jewish New Year, and concludes ten days later with Yom Kippur, the awesome Day of Atonement. This entire period is a time for introspection, self-evaluation, self-examination.

The mood of these days is contrite and sober. How could it be otherwise when we focus the spotlight of conscience upon ourselves? Moral inventory, honestly taken, is rarely conducive to heightened self-appreciation.

The gulf between what we could be and what we are, between our vast potentialities and our limited achievements, underscores the need for repentance—a return to God, an upreaching for the Highest. However, the awareness of our sins and our human frailty is relieved by the comforting faith that we can conquer sin. We need not remain the unwilling captives of our transgressions. Given a determined will on our part, we can count on divine assistance to liberate us from the shackles of our own fashioning.

Thus our sages taught: "If a man opens his heart even as slightly as a needle's eye, God will open it as wide as the gateway to the Temple hall" (Canticles Rabbah 5:2). God is not only our judge but also our ally in the struggle for moral regeneration.

By which pathway does the penitent return? How is God's forgiveness acquired? The discipline of repentance consists of three distinct steps.

Initially, there must be the conscious awareness of having sinned. Rationalization, concealment, projection—these and other mental masks we use to disguise our failures must be removed. We need first the courage to accuse ourselves.

The consciousness of sin must be followed by its confession directly to God without benefit of human mediator. Judaism does not empower its clergy to forgive sin. Only God has that power.

Having confessed his sins, the true penitent must determine in his heart of hearts not to repeat the sin. Remorse without resolution is inadequate. True atonement involves amendment.

This then is the threefold spiritual strategy to rid ourselves of sin: recognition, recitation, renunciation. Where the sin is against a fellow man, a fourth step is required: reparation.

"If you have sinned against your brother, go first and appease him, otherwise the Day of Atonement cannot absolve you" (Mishnah Yoma 8:9). If we have taken that which belongs to another, we must return it. If we have offended someone by harsh words or hurtful deeds, we must summon up the strength to ask that person's forgiveness. Only after we have come to terms with one another can we come before God seeking to be reconciled with Him.

When we truly *atone* we become *at one* with one another and with God.

Forgiving Those We Have Injured

Everybody praises forgiveness, but few practice it. The English poet Alexander Pope wrote, "To err is human; to forgive divine," but a revised modern version declares, "To err is human; to forgive, unusual."

The Bible records a noble instance of forgiveness when Joseph is reconciled with his brothers. But even there that forgiveness does not come easily.

Joseph torments his brothers in many cruel ways before he finally reveals his true identity. He then reassures them, "Now, be not grieved nor angry with yourselves, that you sold me hither; for God sent me ahead of you to preserve life. . . . It was not you that sent me here, but God" (Genesis 45:5, 8).

Yes, Joseph does ultimately forgive his brothers. But why does he find it so hard to do so?

Well, we say, because his brothers hurt him. If Reuben had not interceded, they would have killed him. As it was, they stripped him of his beloved coat of many colors, threw him into the pit, and then sold him as a slave. It's not easy to forgive such abuse. But perhaps there was another reason for Joseph's long delay in forgiving his brothers. He may have had trouble forgiving them not because they had wronged him, but because he had wronged them!

Strange as this may sound, it is true that we frequently develop very strong feelings against people whom we have hurt. Long ago, the Roman historian Tacitus wrote, "It is a principle of human nature to hate those whom you have injured." And Joseph Jacobs, a contemporary historian, declared, "The highest and most difficult of all moral lessons is to forgive those we have injured."

In Joseph's case, it was plain that his own inflammatory actions had provoked his brothers' harsh reactions. He had gossiped about them, carried tales about them back to their father, had dreams about lording it over them, and was insensitive enough to tell those dreams to his brothers. And all the while, he strutted around in his coat of many colors—the tantalizing reminder that he was their father's favorite.

Perhaps it was when Joseph finally faced up to this painful truth that he was able to gather enough strength to admit to himself that he had indeed been the offender; then he was able to make peace with his brothers.

Joseph might help us to find our own way to forgiveness. He would urge us to face ourselves honestly and truthfully. We may then be able to forgive those we have injured.

Disturbing the Comfortable

On the Jewish calendar, the summer months are virtually free of any special days. There is one noteworthy exception—Tisha b'Av, the ninth day of the month of Av. On that day, traditional Jews observe a twenty-four-hour fast in commemoration of the destruction of both Jerusalem temples, events that occurred, ironically, on the same day, albeit some six hundred years apart.

The Sabbath immediately following this melancholy anniversary has a special name—"The Sabbath of Comfort." It is so designated because the prophetic portion read in the synagogue on that day begins with the words: "Comfort my people, comfort them, says your God" (Isaiah 40:1).

One of the primary roles of religion in our lives is to provide comfort. Any student of Jewish history knows that the Jews were able to survive the repeated efforts to destroy them because their faith offered them life-sustaining reservoirs of solace and strength.

For all of life's bruises and aches, for the soul's distress and anguish, for grief and loneliness, for disillusionment and despair—for all these afflictions we look to our faith—whatever it may be—for consolation and comfort. But even when we have said all this, we have not yet exhausted the function that religion should perform for us. It should not only comfort us when we are disturbed; it should also disturb us when we are comfortable.

The prophets who could soothe with motherly compassion when their people were heartsick could also scold with bitter condemnation when their people appeared heartless. Isaiah who called out, "Comfort my people, comfort them . . ." was the same prophet who cried out, "Woe unto the rebellious children" (Isaiah 30:1).

I suppose it makes better advertising copy to promote religion as a comforter than as a critic. Who welcomes critics? We already seem to have more than we need. And yet we know in our hearts that when religion offers only peace of mind and a selfish salvation that turns its back on the rest of the world, at that point religion destroys its own highest purposes.

120

In these difficult times, religion should be a disturber of the peace, a goad to conscience, and the source of a blazing sense of restlessness to redress the world's wrongs. In a world where two-thirds of its inhabitants worry about eating at all while the remaining third worry about eating too much; where terrorists pass themselves off as "freedom fighters"; where powerful countries publish and distribute hate literature; where men and women languish in prison for the crimes of exercising free speech or of wanting to emigrate; where nations buy missiles and tanks before they build hospitals and schools; where four out of every five people live under a dictatorship—in such a world, religion should be a disturber of the peace.

Religion can serve us best today not by encouraging our complacency but by shattering it. "Noble discontent," it has been said, "is the path to heaven." It is also a good way to walk the earth.

What Faith Cannot Do

The word *faith* is widely used as a synonym for "religion." Thus we might refer to a Christian as a "member of the Christian faith." A Jew is often described as belonging "to the Jewish faith." Thus, "faith" and "religion" are so intimately related that a clergyman is expected to extol the power of faith and to expound on what faith can do for us. So, for a change, perhaps it might be helpful to think about those things that faith cannot do for us. If we are not to abuse our faith or misuse it, we ought to be aware of its limitations.

The first thing that faith cannot do for us is exempt us from thinking. To believe does not mean to suspend our critical faculties. Tertullian, the third-century religious writer, uttered the famous statement: "I believe because it is absurd." The queen in Lewis Carroll's *Through the Looking Glass* has the same conception of what it means to believe. When she tells Alice that she is one hundred and one years, five months, and one day old, Alice says, "I cannot believe that." "Can't you?" says the queen. "Try again. Draw a long breath and shut your eyes."

No, true faith does not require us to believe the absurd or to shut our eyes to the realities of life, the discoveries of science, or the evidence of reason. Albert Einstein put it accurately: "Science without religion is lame; religion without science is blind." Moreover, those who believe absurdities will practice atrocities. One of God's greatest gifts to us is the power of reason, and when we use it properly we pay highest tribute to Him who, in the words of our prayer book, "mercifully endows the human being with understanding."

In the second place, faith cannot exempt us from toil. To believe in God does not mean to sit back and wait for Him to do for us what we must do for ourselves. An old adage offers sound advice: "Trust in God but row away from the rocks."

Faith is not meant to be a narcotic but a stimulant; it is a call to action, not a substitute for it. Faith does not mean "God's in His Heaven, all's right with the world." It does mean God who is in

Heaven urges us to work with Him in righting what is wrong with the world.

Lastly, faith cannot exempt us from trouble. It does not shield us against sorrow or suffering. Our belief in God grants us no immunity against cancer or heart disease or death on the highway.

How often have I heard people say: "When my mother died, I stopped believing in God." "He was such a good person. Why did this tragedy happen to him?"

Many of us have a faith that shrinks when it is washed in the waters of adversity. We forget that trouble and sorrow have a passkey to every home in the land; no one is exempt from suffering. To believe in God does not mean that we and those who are dear to us will be spared those burdens that are the common lot of all of us.

To believe in Him does mean that we should live by His commandments so that our deeds bring no harvest of pain, remorse, or fear. Our faith should also give us the strength to go on in the face of adversity and the understanding that we may even emerge from our trials wiser and more humane because of what we have endured.

Spiritual Indigestion

The prophet Jeremiah was involved in one of history's most risky real-estate deals. The piece of land in question was in Jerusalem, and what made the purchase so speculative was the timing. You see, the year was 587 B.C.E. and Jerusalem was under an unbreakable siege by the powerful Babylonian armies. The destruction of the city and the exile of its inhabitants was imminent. Indeed, Jeremiah himself had predicted these events and had gotten himself thrown into prison for his efforts.

At this perilous time, God advises Jeremiah to purchase a plot of land. Why exactly then? God assures Jeremiah that after destruction and exile there will be rebirth and return, and the fields shall once again be valued property.

But how can Jeremiah convince the people not to despair? How can they be persuaded to cling to so fragile a hope? Only one way—buy a field. Risk some silver and save a people. Jeremiah's faith in the future would be of little consequence unless he acted on that faith.

A vital truth speaks to us from this dramatic transaction: The value of our beliefs is reflected in the way we behave. Our convictions become concrete where they are converted into conduct. Our creeds become vital when they shape our deeds.

A national survey a little while ago revealed that 90 percent of the American people believe in God. It would seem that God never had it so good as in America today. But this same survey also contained the query: "Would you say your religious beliefs have any effect on your practice in business or politics?" To this question a majority answered "No." The respondents said that their religious beliefs had no impact on their daily conduct. For too many of us, religion, while it remains respectable, has become almost totally irrelevant.

These figures justify the complaint of Dr. Melvin F. Wheatley, a modern clergyman and author, who wrote, "Great hosts of people worship a God of religion who is not at all the God of all life. He is a pious presence in the sacraments but an impudent intruder

124

in the science lab. He is a point of reference for prayers but an unemployed consultant on business contracts."

Dr. Wheatley lays bare one of the deep-rooted maladies of our time, one that is closely related to our widespread anxieties and emotional ailments. We are split spiritual personalities. We swear allegiance to one set of principles and live by another.

We extol self-control and practice self-indulgence.

We proclaim brotherhood and harbor prejudice.

We laud character but strive to climb to the top at any cost.

We erect houses of worship, but our shrines are our places of business and recreation.

We are suffering from a distressing cleavage between the truths we affirm and the values we live by. Our souls are the battle-grounds for civil wars, but we are trying to live serene lives in houses divided against themselves.

It was Harold Laski, the British writer and political theorist, who warned that "the surest way to bring about the destruction of a civilization is to allow the abyss to widen between the values men praise and the values they permit to operate." We overlook this warning at our peril.

Religion, if it is to remain a viable, living thing, must be acted out in the arena of life. Its concern is not only to keep the Sabbath holy but to keep the weekdays honest.

When I was studying for the rabbinate at the Jewish Theological Seminary, one of our teachers cautioned us that the feast of the sermon is always followed by spiritual indigestion unless it is followed by religious exercise. And then he added, "Remember, one kind act will teach more love of God than a thousand sermons."

The matter was summed up best by a prophet whose literary remains are only three chapters in the Bible. He placed us in his everlasting debt when he wrote the three Hebrew words that are translated: "The righteous shall live by his faith" (Habakkuk 2:4).

Preventive Religion

In humorous Jewish folklore, the town of Chelm in Poland was populated by simpletons.

On one occasion, the inhabitants of Chelm called an emergency meeting to consider a serious problem. It seemed that the only road to Chelm climbed up a steep cliff; it was narrow and full of curves. People were always falling off and getting hurt. What to do?

For six days and six nights they deliberated, then they reached a decision. They would build a hospital at the foot of the cliff!

We smile condescendingly at the foolishness of these people, but perhaps we are not so superior after all. Too often we fail to build fences to keep people from falling and instead build hospitals to mend them after they have been hurt.

Several years ago, on the eve of his execution for a well-publicized crime, a doomed criminal was interviewed by a newspaper reporter. One of the things he said evoked genuine sympathy: "If in my childhood I had been paid one percent of the attention I am now getting, I wouldn't be going to the chair."

When Harry Truman was president, he admitted that our nation spent one-twentieth of 1 percent as much on international agencies working for peace as it spent for war. Pennies for fences, millions for hospitals.

Too many of our resources are spent to correct things that should not have happened and could have been prevented.

Preventive medicine is cheaper in every way than curative medicine. Preventing fires costs less than paying for the ravages of carelessness. Preventing family breakups is infinitely less expensive than picking up the pieces after the wreck.

Properly understood, the role of religion is not so much to pick us up after we have fallen as it is to keep us from falling in the first place. To be sure, it is important to know that no moral defeat need be final, but together with the power to repent after wrongdoing, religion offers us the strength to prevent wrongdoing in the first place.

Religion helps us to develop a rich reservoir of spiritual resources, a firm commitment to a life disciplined by the commandments, and an awareness of what God expects of us. These are the fences on life's steep cliffs.

It has been said that the difference between a clever man and a wise man is that the clever man knows how to get out of a predicament the wise man would never have gotten into in the first place.

The Bible puts it simply: "When you build a new house, erect a fence around your roof" (Deuteronomy 22:8).

Give Me the Facts

A famous television detective would begin his investigation by saying: "Give me the facts. Just give me the facts." He would then take those bare facts and reconstruct the crime that had been committed.

Despite our celebrated sleuth's skillful use of the facts, the fact is that facts alone are not enough on which to build a philosophy of life. What is decisive is what we do with the facts of life, how we interpret them, what meaning we see in them.

A dramatic biblical illustration of this truth is found in the celebrated espionage mission Moses launched in the wilderness. He sent a dozen men, one each from the twelve tribes of Israel, to infiltrate the land of Canaan and study the possibility of subduing it. The twelve performed their sensitive mission and returned with their reports. They all surveyed the same land, observed the same people, evaluated the same conditions, and came back with two diametrically opposite conclusions. Ten said that there was no way they could conquer the land. Two said they could indeed accomplish this objective. So here we have it. The same set of facts, but oh, what different conclusions!

The fundamental truth about us is that we see facts not as they are but as we are. Experience is not what happens to us but how we perceive and react to what happens to us. The same facts will produce totally different reactions in different people.

A shoe company, we are told, sent two salesmen to explore the market potential for their product in Africa. After several weeks of investigation, one salesman wired back: "Nobody wears shoes. Consumer demand is zero. The situation is hopeless."

The other salesman wired back an entirely different message: "Nobody wears shoes. Demand limitless. No competition. The situation is fantastic." Same facts—different interpretations.

A much more serious and fateful illustration of this truth was provided by the reactions of various people to the Nazi nightmare. When postwar Germans were asked why they did not help their Jewish fellow citizens, many of them answered, "What could we do?" When the Danish people who risked their lives to save their Jewish countrymen were asked why they helped them, they answered, "What else could we do?" Same facts—different interpretations.

You see, we human beings not only react, we also respond, and the measure of a human being is to be found in the nature of that response. Any clergyman can cite from his personal experience so many illustrations of people whom sorrow made bitter. He can also cite as many or more illustrations of people whom sorrow made better.

There are people who emerge from an encounter with grief richer human beings, taller in stature, more compassionate, more sensitive, more appreciative of the gift of life. They can then say with the poet William Wordsworth: "A deep distress hath humanized my soul."

The same fire that melts the butter hardens the egg. The same wind that extinguishes a match will fan a flame into a stronger blaze. Man does not live by facts alone.

An aggressive atheist in a mood to advertise his point of view painted these words on a roadside billboard: "God is nowhere." A seven-year-old girl riding in the family car passed the billboard. She was thrilled and excited, for she read these words: "God is now here."

Where Serenity Is Found

Phidias, the Greek sculptor, was once commissioned to fashion a statue that would stand high in the temple with its back against the wall. He worked on the entire statue with meticulous care as he strove to make it as perfect as he could.

A friend asked him why he paid so much attention to the back of the statue since it would not be seen by the onlooker. Phidias answered, "The statue must be perfect everywhere because the gods see everywhere."

Phidias's concern with the hidden part of the statue was anticipated by the Hebrew Bible. When the ancient Israelites journeyed through the desert en route to the Promised Land, they were commanded to build a portable tabernacle, a visible reminder of God's presence in their midst.

The tabernacle was to contain an ark built of acacia wood covered with pure gold outside and inside (Exodus 25:10–11). The outside gold was, of course, quite visible, but the inside gold was concealed from view. And gold in the desert was an enormously rare and expensive metal.

The ancient rabbis reflecting on these verses saw in the construction of the ark a vital lesson for the building of our lives: We must strive to be on the inside what we appear to be on the outside. The part of us that is not visible to the onlooker should be fashioned with the same skillful attention as the visible part of us. Gold outside *and* inside!

This is a lesson that merits frequent repetition in our time because it is not overly popular. There is huge concern with how we look on the outside and massive indifference to what we are on the inside.

The commercials targeted to us exploit our concern with the impression we make on others. We are constantly harangued about the whiteness of our teeth, the smoothness of our skin, the texture of our hair, the closeness of the shave, the fit of our clothes.

This preoccupation with appearances was reflected in a sign, seen recently in front of an auto repair shop, that announced: "Wanted: Mechanic with an honest face." Gold on the outside . . .

Perhaps our widespread failure to find contentment and fulfillment may be traceable to this distortion that has crept into our lives. We have been misled into believing that these precious goals are available over the counter, that they can be acquired without effort, without self-discipline and self-mastery. We are discovering to our dismay the inescapable truth of the ancient wisdom—material affluence amid spiritual poverty cannot lead to life abundant.

English critic and editor Middleton Murry's words are worth thinking about:

> When a man is sure that all he wants is happiness, then, most grievously, he deceives himself. All men desire happiness, but they want something different, compared to which happiness is trivial, and in the absence of which happiness turns to dust and ashes in the mouth. There are many names for that which men need—the one thing needful—but the simplest is wholeness.

The basic truth about us is that we cannot find any kind of serenity as long as there is an abyss between what we are and what we pretend to be. We may succeed in fooling all the people all the time, and we can fool ourselves some of the time, but we cannot fool ourselves all the time.

There is within each of us a hunger for integrity; and as long as that hunger is not satisfied, we cannot be at peace with ourselves. No new hairdo or new outfit can answer the yearning for wholeness within. If the well is giving rusty water, it doesn't help to paint the pump.

At the end of Plato's dialogue *Phaedrus,* Socrates prayed: "Make the outer and the inner man one!" At the point in a person's life when that prayer is answered, then he or she finds peace and serenity.

Things That Do Not Change

Someone has objected to the popular adage that "love makes the world go round." He insists that love only keeps the world populated. It is change that makes the world go round.

I believe it was the ancient Greek philosopher Heraclitus who emphasized the idea that things are always in a state of flux. Change is the only constant. Therefore, he said, a man cannot step into the same stream twice. By the time he steps into the stream a second time, both he and the stream have changed.

One of the most striking characteristics of our century has been the intensified rate of change in almost every aspect of our lives. My grandfather grew up in the oxcart age. His grandson is living in the space age. A few years ago, Robert Oppenheimer, the atomic scientist, declared that 90 percent of today's scientific knowledge has been discovered since he left college.

It is exciting to be alive in a time of change. All sorts of wondrous possibilities lie before us. But it is also bewildering to be living in a time of revolutionary change. Familiar landmarks are obliterated and with them there is lost, too, a sense of orientation.

What happens to the old standards of decency? Are they now outmoded? What happens to the ancient teachings about honesty, morality, and human responsibility? Have they become archaic? What value do the old signposts have if people now fly at thirty thousand feet above the roads?

The prophet Isaiah seemed to be pondering such questions even in his day. To be sure, his age was scarcely as volatile as our own. To him, however, it must have seemed to be a time of radical transformation. And so he said to his people, in the name of God: "For the mountains may depart and the hills be removed; but My kindness shall not depart from you, neither shall My covenant of peace be removed, says the Lord who has compassion on you" (Isaiah 54:10).

To the prophet, the mountains and the hills represented the most enduring of physical things. But more enduring than the physical things, he said, are the spiritual values of life—God's kindness and God's promises. These are the changeless realities in a changing world; these are the things one could cling to in a slippery time, the things that the teeth of time would not chew to pieces.

What are some of these things? The redeeming power of compassion, the healing power of forgiveness, the transforming power of love—these things do not change.

The purifying power of repentance, the energizing power of prayer, the sustaining power of faith—these things do not change.

The nourishment that comes from beauty, the strength that comes from adversity, the joy that comes from generosity—these things do not change.

The supreme value of character, the ultimate worth of human life, the permanent perpetuation of personality—these things do not change.

Our capacity to change and improve ourselves, our ability to change the world for the better—these things do not change.

Living at a time of accelerated change, we need desperately the wisdom to cling to the things that do not change.

Things We Can Always Count On

Two days before his untimely death, Pope John Paul I interviewed a fifth-grader in front of some ten thousand people at his weekly general audience.

"Do you always want to be in the fifth grade?" the pontiff asked.

"Yes," the youngster replied, "so I don't have to change teachers."

The audience greeted this answer with loud laughter, but I suspect there was as much honesty as humor in the lad's spontaneous reply.

The truth about us is that every change is upsetting and even traumatic in varying degrees. Deep within each of us is some measure of the fifth-grader's anxiety at the prospect of change. Courage has correctly been defined as the power to let go of the familiar.

The four-year-old clinging to her mother who has just brought her to her first nursery class needs this courage. The nine-year-old en route to his first overnight camp, waving a reluctant good-bye as he fights back the tears, needs this courage.

The adolescent waiting for the boyfriend who is taking her on her first date; the parent marrying off a child; the widow who must now live alone after forty years of shared intimacy—all need the courage to cope with these changes.

We live at a time of massive change. The twentieth century has witnessed more change than all the previous centuries combined. The automobile, the telephone, the radio, the airplane, the television, the computer have profoundly revolutionized our style and pace of living. And even our values, our morality, and our religious beliefs and practices have not been unmoved by the howling winds of change.

At a time like this we need to be reminded of the things that never change. In the words of Ahab in *Moby-Dick,* we "like to feel something in this slippery world that can hold."

The words of the prophet Isaiah seem especially meant for us:

"For the mountains may depart, and the hills be moved, but My kindness shall not depart from you" (Isaiah 54:10).

It is part of the kindness of God that amid all the change there are things we can always count on. The unfailing regularity of the seasons and the reliability of nature; "the glory of the stars, the innocence of morning"; the healing power of time and the sustaining power of hope; the heart's yearning for love and the soul's hunger for prayer; the endless quest for truth and the stubborn struggle for justice; the restless urge to create and the valiant will to overcome—these are some of the things we can count on. These are the things that hold in a slippery world.

Let Us Treasure Our Mona Lisas

In her *Book of Useless Information,* Barbara Cortland tells us that when the *Mona Lisa* was stolen from the Louvre in Paris in 1911 and was missing for two years, more people went to stare at the blank space in the museum than had gone to look at the masterpiece in the twelve previous years.

Far from being "useless," this intriguing bit of information tells us something important about ourselves. It points to our all-too-human tendency to fail to take adequate note of precious things while we have them. But let one of them be taken from us and we become painfully aware of the "blank space" in our lives, and our attention is sharply focused on that "blank space."

The walls of our lives are crowded with *Mona Lisa*s, but we are unmindful of them. Countless blessings attend us daily and we are so insensitive to them.

The more often and the more regularly we receive any blessing, the less likely we are to be aware of it. What is constantly granted is easily taken for granted.

"I have often thought," Helen Keller wrote, "that it would be a blessing if each human being were stricken blind and deaf for a few days at some time during his adult life. Darkness would make him more appreciative of sight; silence would teach him the joys of sound."

Too often it takes a serious threat to our blessings to make us aware of them.

The newspapers reported a touching story of a mother who was taking her young son to Salt Lake City on a melancholy mission. The boy had lost the sight of one eye several years before, and in the intervening years doctors had tried valiantly to save his remaining eye.

Now they had come to the reluctant conclusion that the eye could not be saved. Before the darkness set in, his mother wanted the boy to have a fond, lingering look at the majestic mountains of Utah so that he could take that splendid image with him into the sightless future.

Can we read such a story without becoming acutely aware of the myriad *Mona Lisas* that constantly beckon to us and that we persistently overlook?

The words that Frances Gunther wrote in her Afterword to *Death Be Not Proud*, after the death of her teenage son, are filled with poignant wisdom:

All the wonderful things in life are so simple that one is not aware of their wonder until they are beyond touch. Never have I felt the wonder and beauty and joy of life so keenly as now in my grief that Johnny is not here to enjoy them.

Today when I see parents impatient or tired or bored with their children, I wish I could say to them, "But they are alive, think of the wonder of that! They may be a care and a burden, but think, they are alive! You can touch them—what a miracle!"

All the parents who have lost a child will feel what I mean. Others, luckily, cannot. But I hope they will embrace them with a little added rapture and a keener awareness of joy.

Too many of us look upon prayer exclusively as an effort to obtain blessings we do not have and would like to possess. We forget that one of the primary functions of prayer is to make us gratefully aware of the blessings we already possess and too frequently fail to notice.

Let us treasure our *Mona Lisas* while we may.

How Life Grows Great

He had drunk more than he could tolerate, and the excess of alcohol had dissolved his inhibitions and unsteadied him. As he staggered along the street, he swung his arms with careless abandon until his fist made heavy contact with the face of a passerby.

"What goes on here?" cried the stunned victim.

"This is a free country. I have a right to swing my arms," our inebriated friend protested.

"Yes," agreed the assaulted pedestrian, "but your rights end where my nose begins."

The offender was probably in no condition to absorb that lesson in the true meaning of freedom, but we who enjoy the blessings of liberty cannot afford to disregard the inescapable truth that freedom has its limits. If liberty is not to degenerate into license, there must be restraints. We have to know where the other fellow's nose begins.

The ancient Israelites heard this message quite soon after they gained their freedom. After centuries of enslavement in Egypt, they were finally liberated from backbreaking and soul-suffocating bondage. Free at last! Now they could do whatever they wanted, whenever they wanted.

If this was what they thought, they were soon disabused of this illusion. They were gone from Egypt only a few weeks when they found themselves at the foot of a quaking Mount Sinai and heard the majestic voice out of the heights proclaiming a host of restraints on their freedom: Thou shalt do this! Thou shalt not do that! Do! Don't!

That was freedom?

But of course! That was and is exactly what freedom involves. Before we can do all the things that freedom entitles us to do, we must understand what freedom does not entitle us to do: We are not free to deceive or malign; we are not free to steal or murder; we are not free to discard moral values or encroach upon our neighbor's freedom.

This is not a popular doctrine. We don't like limits on our freedom. We resent repressions and restraints. This is especially true in a time of open rebellion against traditional standards of morality and decency, when "doing your own thing" is a dominant creed.

But, like it or not, a life uncontrolled is a life that will be denied meaningful achievement. A wise teacher reminds us: "No horse ever gets anywhere until it is harnessed. No steam or gas ever drives anything until it is confined. No Niagara is ever turned into light and power until it is tunneled. No life ever grows great until it is dedicated, focused, disciplined."

The middle stanza of "America the Beautiful" says it best:

> *America! America!*
> *God mend thine every flaw.*
> *Confirm thy soul in self-control,*
> *Thy liberty in law!*

We Do Not Know How Soon It Will Be Too Late

A very successful benefactor was interviewed upon his retirement after long years crowded with many notable achievements. He was asked how he managed to accomplish so much. His answer was simple: "I did everything promptly." His career was a living illustration of a truth distilled from an ancient biblical practice.

When the ancient Israelite brought the first fruits of his fields to the Temple in Jerusalem as a gift to God, the offering was accompanied, as a requirement of his faith, by a verbal expression of gratitude. In the course of that declaration, he reviewed God's kindness to his ancestors and to himself. Then he concluded with these words: "And now, behold, I have brought the first of the fruit of the land, which You, O Lord, have given me" (Deuteronomy 26:10). The rabbis called sharp attention to the words *and now* and deduced from them the importance of promptness in fulfilling the commandment. We may not delay in discharging our obligation to God. It is to be done "now."

Our sages were human, and they knew only too well our tendency to put off until tomorrow those things we already have put off until today. They knew that nothing was easier than not to find the time to do those things we do not want to do. But they knew, too, that putting off any easy thing made it difficult and that putting off a hard one made it impossible. And so they stressed the urgency of the *now*.

The intervening centuries have done nothing to blunt the sharp edge of their penetrating truth. It touches us at many vital points in our lives. We are all too often like the undisciplined young man who prayed to God to make him better, but he prayed softly for fear that God might hear him and answer his prayer too soon. Like too many of us, he wanted to discharge his obligations with a dated check.

We will be good, O God, but please do not press us too hard. We need more time. We will become honest in our business, but not right now. First we have to take care of all our needs—real and

140

imaginary. We will spend more time with our children when economic pressures are lighter and other obligations fewer. We will start coming to worship for weekly renewal and some interior redecorating, but not right now. When we retire—yes, then we will have plenty of time.

Oh, the things we are going to do when we have time—the classes we will join, the services we will render, the passions we will conquer. We live in a world that gives us one day at a time without any assurance of tomorrow. We do not know how soon it will be too late. But today is ours to do all the good things for which this day was made, the things that need doing *now*.

Thanks for What's Not Lost

A few years ago the nineteen-year-old son of the president of Cyprus was kidnapped by terrorists who threatened to behead him unless his father agreed to release several of their jailed comrades. In a remarkable display of fortitude, the father refused to submit to the kidnappers' demands, and after four tension-filled days the young man was released unharmed.

When he returned to his family, his mother jubilantly exclaimed, "This is the happiest day of my life!"

Good people everywhere, and especially parents, can understand the mother's unbounded joy. Her son had been snatched from the jaws of death! She had come so close to losing him!

However, as we think about the mother's jubilant reaction, a question rises in our minds. What did the mother have after her son was returned that she did not have five days earlier, before he was kidnapped? In what way was she richer? Why was she so much happier than before? We know the answer, of course. What she now had was a profoundly deepened sense of appreciation for a blessing she almost lost. Only when the life of her son was severely threatened did she realize how vastly she cherished that life.

Every one of us is like that mother: It often takes a serious threat to our blessings to make us aware of them. And, sadly, sometimes we do not value them until they are gone beyond retrieving.

Channing Pollock, in his essay "The Secret of Being Rich," made this pertinent observation: "I should not be the only one to laugh if I stopped in the street to voice gratitude for the air we breathe. But if they could hear me, there would be no merriment from the men who died in sunken submarines or damaged mines or in the Black Hole of Calcutta."

The fact is, of course, that if we were asked to draw up a list of our assets, we would probably never think of mentioning such things as our vision, our limbs, our sanity, our ability to eat and to speak. Everyone has that, we say. Well, on second thought, almost everyone.

But would we be willing to exchange any of these blessings for all those things we want so badly that they fill us with discontent and rob us of a sense of gratefulness?

A worthwhile Thanksgiving Day exercise might consist of sitting down with two sheets of paper. On one we might list all the things we crave and are yearning to acquire. On the other sheet we would enumerate all those things we have and could lose. To our surprise, we would find the first list quickly exhausted while the second would appear endless. We would probably soon tear up the first list feeling a little ashamed and largely thankful.

We might then understand better the meaning of the prayer:

Thou has given so much to me. Give me one thing more—a grateful heart.

The Search for More Abundant Life

One of the distinctive, traditional synagogue practices is the public reading of a portion of the Torah, or Pentateuch. This is done no fewer than four times during the ordinary week. Should a Jewish festival occur during the week, the Torah would be read on those days too.

The most joyous of all Jewish festivals is Simchat Torah—"Rejoicing in the Torah." On that day the reading of Deuteronomy, the last of the Five Books of Moses, is completed; immediately thereafter we begin again the reading of Genesis, the first book of the Torah. Thus the reading of the Torah is never really finished. It continues uninterrupted.

And so does our obligation to study it. We are never relieved of that happy privilege.

Perhaps the greatest tribute to continuous Torah study was spoken by a first-century sage: "Turn it again and again, for everything is in it; contemplate it, grow gray and old over it, and swerve not from it, for there is no greater good" (Mishnah Abot 2:14).

Judaism is vitally concerned that we serve God with heart, soul, and might. But it has been no less insistent that we serve Him too with our minds—with minds that stay open and keep growing.

Someone has said that some minds are like concrete: all mixed up and permanently set. As we grow older, it is very tempting to develop a permanent mind set. But minds, like parachutes, are valuable only when open.

To shut the windows of the mind is to court mental and spiritual suffocation. Leonardo da Vinci, who lived to a ripe old age and continued to paint masterpieces into old age, declared, "Learning keeps the soul young and decreases the bitterness of old age." We must literally never stop going to school, broadening our horizons, and expanding our knowledge.

This is the distinctive Jewish contribution to mental hygiene—the unparalleled emphasis upon study as a process that only death ought to terminate.

Judah bar Ilai, a second-century sage, deeply impressed a

pagan in the marketplace by his radiant face. "This man," said the pagan, "must either be intoxicated or he has just discovered a hidden treasure."

Rabbi Judah overheard him and said: "Friend, I do not drink except when I must for ritual purposes. Neither have I found any treasure. I am a poor man."

"Then what makes your face shine so?"

"That is quite simple," Rabbi Judah answered. "I study all the time, and the quest for knowledge makes the face of a man to shine."

As long as we keep our minds open and alert, as long as we are willing to try a new skill, entertain a new thought, develop a new friend, surrender an old prejudice—so long do we remain vital people, so long do we gain ground and move forward in the search for more abundant life.

Why Not Me?

"Never volunteer!" was the first bit of barracks wisdom usually passed along to the new army recruit by the veteran. A corollary of this advice was: "Don't stick your neck out."

This counsel is not confined to the military. A host of people who never wore the uniform have made "Never volunteer" the golden rule of their lives. This all-too-human trait prompted this lament from a colleague:

> *There's a clever young fellow named*
> SOMEBODY ELSE,
> *There's nothing this fellow can't do.*
> *He's busy from morning 'till late at night*
> *Just substituting for you.*
> *You're asked to do this, or asked*
> *to do that,*
> *And what is your ready reply?*
> *"Get* SOMEBODY ELSE, *Mr. Chairman,*
> *He'll do it much better than I."*

Some of us "never volunteer" because of shyness, others because of selfishness, and still others because of a sense of inferiority.

Whatever the reason for our relying on Somebody Else, we can be enormously encouraged by the bold example of the prophet Isaiah. There was a most unpleasant assignment on hand—to speak words of harsh rebuke to his own people. This was hardly a task to enhance his popularity among his neighbors.

And then he heard an insistent voice asking: "Whom shall I send, and who will go for us?" Isaiah answered simply: "Here am I; send me" (Isaiah 6:8-9).

There's something so reassuring in those simple words: "Here am I; send me." How they shore up our faith in the ability of man to respond to the challenge to rise above himself! Most of the good that gets done would remain undone if there weren't decent people responding: "Here am I; send me."

In Kibbutz Ashdot Yaakov, in the north of Israel, there is a shoemaker who holds two Ph.D. degrees from European universities. Why did he come to Israel some forty years ago?

"One day," he answers, "I was telling somebody about the need to 'conquer' the land around the Sea of Galilee, cleanse it of malaria, make it fruitful. Suddenly, I thought: 'Why not me?' So I went. And all my life I have kept on trying to ask myself, 'Why not me?' "

The glory of the human race are those who ask "Why not me?" when there is great work to be done—visiting the sick, comforting the bereaved, feeding the hungry, cheering the distressed, fighting for truth, protesting injustice, advancing worthy causes.

These people not only bring blessings; they are blessed. For unless we live in some measure for others, we hardly live at all.

CHRISTIAN HERALD ASSOCIATION AND ITS MINISTRIES

CHRISTIAN HERALD ASSOCIATION, founded in 1878, publishes The Christian Herald Magazine, one of the leading interdenominational religious monthlies in America. Through its wide circulation, it brings inspiring articles and the latest news of religious developments to many families. From the magazine's pages came the initiative for CHRISTIAN HERALD CHILDREN'S HOME and THE BOWERY MISSION, two individually supported not-for-profit corporations.

CHRISTIAN HERALD CHILDREN'S HOME, established in 1894, is the name for a unique and dynamic ministry to disadvantaged children, offering hope and opportunities which would not otherwise be available for reasons of poverty and neglect. The goal is to develop each child's potential and to demonstrate Christian compassion and understanding to children in need.

Mont Lawn is a permanent camp located in Bushkill, Pennsylvania. It is the focal point of a ministry which provides a healthful "vacation with a purpose" to children who without it would be confined to the streets of the city. Up to 1000 children between the ages of 7 and 11 come to Mont Lawn each year.

Christian Herald Children's Home maintains year-round contact with children by means of an *In-City Youth Ministry*. Central to its philosophy is the belief that only through sustained relationships and demonstrated concern can individual lives be truly enriched. Special emphasis is on individual guidance, spiritual and family counseling and tutoring. This follow-up ministry to inner-city children culminates for many in financial assistance toward higher education and career counseling.

THE BOWERY MISSION, located at 227 Bowery, New York City, has since 1879 been reaching out to the lost men on the Bowery, offering them what could be their last chance to rebuild their lives. Every man is fed, clothed and ministered to. Countless numbers have entered the 90-day residential rehabilitation program at the Bowery Mission. A concentrated ministry of counseling, medical care, nutrition therapy, Bible study and Gospel services awakens a man to spiritual renewal within himself.

These ministries are supported solely by the voluntary contributions of individuals and by legacies and bequests. Contributions are tax deductible. Checks should be made out either to CHRISTIAN HERALD CHILDREN'S HOME or to THE BOWERY MISSION.

Administrative Office: 40 Overlook Drive, Chappaqua, New York 10514
Telephone: (914) 769-9000